THE LAST DAYS

THE DEPTH OF THE BOOK OF REVELATION

or

The last days

Praying that its exposition

May meet with His divine

Approval and Blessings

AS

THE LAST PROPHETIC BOOK
OF HOLY SCRIPTURE

BY

Dr. WILLIAM N. GLOVER, S.T.D.

AUTHOR OF A BOOK ON
DISPENSATIONAL TRUTH

ENTITLED

"FROM ETERNITY TO ETERNITY"

THE
LAST DAYS
A GUIDE TO UNDERSTANDING THE BOOK OF REVELATION

DR. WILLIAM N. GLOVER, S.T.D

THE LAST DAYS
A GUIDE TO UNDERSTANDING THE BOOK OF REVELATION
Copyright © 2016 William Glover.

THE HOLY BIBLE, NEW INTERNTIONAL VERSION, NIV COPYRIGHT Biblica, inc. used by permission. All rights reserved worldwide.

St. John 16: 3, reads: "They will do such things because they have not known the Father or me." (NIV.)

All scriptures quoted from the "New International version of the Bible" will look as follows "(NIV.)" All Others Quotes from the Bible will be from the Kings James Version of the Bible.

Scripture taken from the King James Version of the Bible.

iUniverse books may be ordered through booksellers or by contacting:

iUniverse
1663 Liberty Drive
Bloomington, IN 47403
www.iuniverse.com
1-800-Authors (1-800-288-4677)

ISBN: 978-1-4917-9988-8 (sc)
ISBN: 978-1-4917-9989-5 (e)

Library of Congress Control Number: 2016910068

Print information available on the last page.

iUniverse rev. date: 06/21/2016

CONTENTS

REFERENCES

Most references in this book are Scriptural; and the Scriptural references are from the following Books:

King James Version of the Bible

The Holy Bible, New International Version*, NIV* Copyright, 1973, 1978, 1984. By Biblica, Inc. Used by permission of Zondervan.

All rights reserved Worldwide.

The following books were used for other references:

Unger's Bible Dictionary (Moody Press)

The Expanded Panorama Bible Study Course (Alfred T. Eade S.T.D.)

The Book of Revelation Illustrated (Clarence LARKIN)

African Presence in the Bible (Wyatt Tee Walker)

From Eternity To Eternity (William N. Glover S.T.D.)

Commentary on the Whole Bible (Matthew Henry).

THE REVELATION
OF JESUS CHRIST

The character of the book of Revelation is described by its title. It is not the revelation of St. John the Apostle, but the Revelation of Jesus Christ.

The revelation which God gave unto Jesus Christ, to show unto His servants things which must shortly come to pass; and He sent and signified it by His Angel unto His servant.

John the Apostle; received the word of God, and of the testimony of Jesus Christ, and of all things that he saw. However, the book is endorsed by Jesus Himself in Rev. 22:16, and Rev. 22: 13 let's us know who is actually during the testifying.

The word Revelation is a form of the Greek word "APOCALUPSIS" meaning "TO UNVEIL"; that portion of the Greek word "APO" means "away from" and the Greek word "KALUMMA" means "a veil", Hence Revelation means taking away of a veil. It is not so much a revelation or unveiling of the person of Christ, however, it does disclose His High Priestly and Kingly glory, because it is the unveiling of those events that shall precede and accompany His return to the earth.

What is revealed in the book of Revelation, was given unto Jesus Christ, by God the Father, to show unto His servants the "**things which would shortly come to pass.**" And which is now coming to pass? The book of Revelation is a Prophetic book as well as a Symbolic book, because it is written mostly in symbolic type language, thus the statement---"He sent and SIGNIFIED IT BY His angels unto His servant John." In this interpretation the interest is from a futurist standpoint. Chapters two and three covers the present Church Dispensation of Grace. From chapter four to the end of the book is all future. (future meaning before the return of Christ to the earth.) The purpose of this book is to show that the book of Revelation is to be taken literally, and that it is written in chronological order. (Arranged in order of time of occurrence.) Deut. 29:29 says' that "The secrect things belong unto the Lord our God, but those things which are **"REVEALED"** belong unto us and our children forever. The Salutation can be found in chapter 1: 4-6; (The Salutation is the greetings) it is addressed to the "Seven churches which are in Asia Minor" By Asia, it does not mean the entire Continent of Asia, or even the whole of Asia Minor, but only the western end of Asia Minor bordering on the Aegean and Mediterranean Seas, and about the size of the State of Pennsylvania There were other Churches in Asia Minor; but these seven Churches undoubtedly, were representative or typical Churches, chosen for certain characteristics; typical of the character of the Church of Christ, not only in that day, but on down the centuries until the Church shall be removed from the earth, and represent seven Church periods that will be clearly defined in Church History.

In the Benediction---"Grace be unto you, and peace, from Him which is, and was, and is to come; and from the seven Spirits which are before His throne; and from Jesus Christ, who is the Faithful witness,…" we behold the Trinity. Here Jesus is distinguished from…" HIM (the Father) which IS, and which Was, and which is to Come," but in verse 8 He claims the same Title, which only proves that Jesus is God manifest in the flesh, and that He and The Father are one.

It is also worthy of note that the "Threefold Office" Jesus as Prophet, Priest, and King is brought out in the Salutation. He is called The "Faithful Witness," as such He is a Prophet. As the "first begotten from the dead," He carried His own blood into the Heavenly Tabernacle, and thus performed the work of a Priest.

As Prophet Jesus is God's Word, as Priest He is God's Lamb, and as King He Is God's LION. John also emphasizes the fact that Jesus Loved us before He Washed (loosed) us from our sins in His own blood, and that He has made us "KINGS" and "PRIESTS" unto God, and that we need no human Priest to stand between us and God.

THE ANNOUNCEMENT: (REV. 1: 7).

This verse refers to the second Stage of Christ's coming, the "Revelation" or "Appearing." The first stage of His coming is the "Rapture," and it is not mention in the book; however it will fulfil Zech. 12: 10, (KJV.} "They (meaning the Jews) shall look upon Me (meaning Jesus) whom they have pierced." This is surely confirmation of the view that the book of Revelation deals mainly with the events that follows after the "Rapture" (after Jesus give's up the sepulcher.) and precedes and attends the "Revelation" or the return to the earth by Jesus.

It is difficult to imagine the grief and remorse that will fill the hearts of those Jews who shall witness the return of the Lord to the Mount of Olives, especially when they shall see in His hands and feet the **"Print of The nails,"** and He shall be revealed as the One they crucified. TheProphet Zechariah in Zech. 12: 10(KJV.) describes it as a time of great **"Bitterness"** and a day of great mourning in Jerusalem, when families will separate themselves from their neighbors and mourn every family apart. And not only shall the Jews mourn because they rejected Him, but will mourn when they realize that He has come back, come back, not as a Saviour, but as a Judge to punish them for their iniquities

FOREWORD

In this book of the "the last days", Dr. Glover presents this fascinating book to us in the most simpless form. He presents it as a book not to be read with fear, **for it is the most feared**, because of its content. This book is about the finality of the world as we know it. For it fore-tells the word of God as to what is to come. He tells us about the choosen people through whom the Messiah would come. This book gives us an appreciation of what God did to redeem us. He discusses the arrival and life of the Messiah and gives us even more confidence in the fact that it is indeed true. He make's it clear that this book stands along in a peculiar kind of way. He lets us know that this book not only tells us about what is happening but explains in understandable terms "**What will happen**." He gives to us what he believe is a way to understand what you read in this book. What he presents in this book helps one to understand the symbolism and the method that God will use to accomplish what is intended in the book of Revelation. Even though it may seem to be complicated, it really is not. Even though it may appear to be scary, it really is not. It is a book which describes events that are going to occur in the order in which they are going to occur for the things that will happen on this earth as we know it. For all of us who believe; this book will solidify our belief in what we've read in the previous books of the Bible. I am prayerful that this book will give you the method to read and understand the book of Revelation which is the most intriguing book in the Bible. **Rev. Dr. Robert Emanuel; Graduate of Ala. State college; Pastor Friendship Prim. Bat. Church. Mobile, Al. ; & ST. Lewis Prim. Bat. Church. Yellow bluff, Al**.

PREFACE

Revelation is the last book of the Bible, the book of futurist unveiling. "This book of Revelation," was written between A.D. 90 thru A.D. 96; on the island of Patmos, in the Aegean Sea. The book is named "Revelation" because it is the revelation of Jesus Christ as given to the Apostle John. The word "Revelation" in the Greek language is "Apocalupsis." It is now called by most "The Apocalypse" the verb form of, to unveil; it is the unveiling of those events that shall precede and accompany Christ's return to the earth. This is seen from the fact that what is revealed in the book of Revelation, was given unto Jesus Christ, by God the Father, to show unto His servants the **"things which must shortly come to pass."** And is now coming to pass in this dispensation of Grace. This dispensation or period began with the death, burial and resurrection of Christ (Rom. 3: 24-26; 4:24-25 (KJV.)). The point of testing is no longer legal obedience to the law as a condition of Salvation, but acceptance or rejection of Christ with good works as the fruit of Salvation (St John 1:12; 3:36(KJV.)); 1 John: 5:10-12 (NIV.)). The predicted end of the testing of man under Grace is the apostasy of the professing Church (II Tim. 3:1-8 (KJV.)) and the subsequent apocalyptic judgments. The book of Revelation is a prophetic book as well as a Symbolic book, because it is written mostly in symbolic type language, thus the statement---"He sent and signified it by His angels unto His servant John." In this interpretation the interest is from a futurist standpoint. Chapters two and three covers that present Church Dispensation. From chapter four to the end of the book are all future. If according to the protestant theory, the Churches are divine-human institutions, and not infallible, then the rule of conduct must be in accordance with the teaching of the infallible word of God. The ethical standard of the visible church must be simply that of the Holy

Scripture, otherwise the true idea of the Church is lost sight of; and the Church assumes either too much or too little. Only by adhering to the word of God as the "rule of faith and practice" can the Churches be saved from the two extremes; one purpose of this book is to show that the book of Revelation is to be taken literally, and that it is written in chronological order; (Arranged in order of time of occurrence.) Revelation Chapter 1:4-6,(KJV.) addresses the "Seven Churches which are in Asia Minor." By Asia, it does not mean the entire continent of Asia, or even the whole of Asia Minor, but only the western end of Asia Minor, bordering on the Aegean and Mediterranean Seas, and about the size of the state of Pennsylvania. There were other Churches in Asia Minor as well; but these seven Churches undoubtedly, were representative or typical Churches, chosen for certain characteristics, that were typical of the character of the Church of Christ. Not only in that day, but on down the centuries until the Church shall be removed from the earth, and represent seven Church periods clearly defined in Church history.

In the benediction "Grace be unto you, and peace from Him which is, and was, and is to come; and from the seven Spirits which are before His throne; and from Jesus Christ, who is the faithful witness;" "**we behold the Trinity.**" Here Jesus is distinguished from Him" (The Father) which is, was, and is to come. But in Revelation 1 Verse 8 Jesus claims the same title, which only proves that Jesus is God, manifest in the flesh, and that He and The Father are one. It is also noteworthy that the "Threefold Office", Jesus as Prophet, Priest, and King is brought out in this Salutation. He is called the "Faithful Witness," and as such He is a Prophet. He is also the "First Begotten from the dead," which means that He carried His own blood into the Heavenly Tabernacle, and thus performed the work of a Priest. As Prophet Jesus is God's Word, as Priest He is God's Lamb, and as King He is God's Lion.

John emphasizes the fact that Jesus Loved us before He washed us from our sins in His own blood, and He has made us "Kings" and "Priest" unto God, and that we need no human priest to stand between us and God. Now Revelation 1 verse 7 refers to the second stage of Christ's coming, the "Revelation" or "Appearing". The first stage of His returning to earth is the "Rapture," even though the word "Rapture" is not mentioned in the book of Revelation; however, it does fulfill Zech. 12:10 "(KJV.) They (The Jews) shall look upon me (Jesus) whom they have pierced." This is surely confirmation of the view that the book of Revelation deals mainly with; the events that follows <u>after</u> the "Rapture" and precedes and attends the "revelation" or Jesus return to the earth. For I Thess. 4:16-17 lets us know that the Lord himself will come down from heaven, with a loud shout. With the voice of the archangel and with the trumpet call of God and the dead in Christ will rise first. After that, we who are still alive and are left will be caught up with them in the clouds to meet the Lord in the air.

It will be very difficult to even imagine the grief and remorse that will fill the hearts of those Jews who shall witness the return of the Lord Jesus Christ to the Mount of Olives; when they shall see in His hands and feet the "**Print of the nails,**" and He shall be revealed as the One they crucified. Zech. 12:10 (KJV.) describes it as a time of great "**Bitterness**" and a day of great mourning in Jerusalem, when families will separate themselves from their neighbors and mourn every family apart. And not only shall the Jews mourn because they rejected Him when He came the first time, but the nations of the earth will mourn when they realize that He has returned, not as a Saviour but a Judge, to punish them for their iniquities.

DR. William N. Glover, S.T.D.

INTRODUCTION

While attending **United Christian College of New York**, *and* **New York Theological Seminary where I received my "Doctor of Sacred Theology Degree"** *I became interested in the "Book of Revelation." As I began to read the various different interpretation, I realized that the average person might have trouble understanding where the Apostle John was coming from.* My aim in writing this book was to present a clear picture of God's intent to give us a futurist understanding as to the revelation which God gave unto Jesus Christ, to show unto His servant's things which must shortly come to pass; and are now coming to pass in this dispensation. So He sent and signified it by His angel unto His servant John the Apostle; who bare record of the word of God, and of the testimony of Jesus Christ, and of all things that he saw. And thus the book of Revelation is endorsed by Jesus Himself in Rev. 22:16.(KJV.)

This book contains none of my opinions, and is not a commentary made up of phrases from other writers. The only Author I have sought to follow is the Author of the book of Revelation, the Lord Jesus Christ Himself.

The book of Revelation is different from all other books, thus revealing its Divine Authorship. It is the only portion of the New Testament to which Jesus Christ gives His endorsement, and affixes His signature, saying at its close; "I Jesus have sent mine Angel to testify unto you these things in the Churches." Rev. 22:16.(NIV.) Thus, the book of Revelation is the revelation of Jesus Christ, which God gave unto **Him**, to show unto His servant's things which must shortly come to pass; and was sent by His angel. But when John fell down to worship the angel, he said, "See thou do it not: for I am thou fellow servant, and of thy brethren the prophets and of them which keeps the saying of this book." Rev. 22:8-9. (That angel

may have been one of the old prophets raised from the dead himself, just for that purpose?)

This book of Revelation is not a history book; it does not record the past, but it does reveal the future. It makes this claim in the title. "Blessed is he that readeth, and they that hear the words of this Prophecy," Rev. 1:3 (KJV.) ; and in the last Chapter, four times. Rev. 22:7, 10, 18, 19. In all of them, unfilled prophecies are fulfilled. In this book of Revelation, all prophecy has been finalized until Jesus returns. There has been no "new revelation" since it was written; anyone claiming to have received new and later "revelations" are impostors and false prophets. There is no place for additions or subtractions in the book of Revelation. It opens promising the reader a "blessing," and ends with a "curse" upon those who "**ADD UNTO**" or "**TAKE FROM**" it. Rev. 1: 3; 22: 18-19. The reference here is to the "reader" and "hearers" of the Scripture as it was read in the Synagogue in the Apostle's day. The book of Revelation being the last prophecy, naturally we would expect it to finalize all previous prophecy, and as all previous prophecy had to do with the CHURCH, ISRAEL, and THE NATIONS, so we should expect this last prophecy to give us the final word explaining the final prophecy's; well, that is what it does. We find the Church in the beginning, Israel in the middle, and the saved Nations at the end. These three are also seen in the construction of the Holy City, New Jerusalem; where we have the Church in the foundation, represented by the names of the twelve Apostles, and Israel in the Gates, with the names of the twelve tribes of Israel written over them, and the Saved Nations in the streets, where they walk in the light of the City's Glory.

When John wrote the book of Revelation as it was given to him in A. D. 95-96 the Christians were undergoing a persecution under the Roman Emperor Domitian, and as a result of this persecution John had been banished to the Isle of Patmos, a small, island in the Aegean Sea 30 miles off the west coast of Asia Minor, and opposite the city of Ephesus.

John was banished for "the word of God, and his testimony of Jesus Christ." John was the Pastor of the Church at Ephesus at the time of his banishment, and it was to that Church that the first message to the seven Churches was addressed. Studies of the entire Bible let us know that both the Old and New Testament speak of the **"Day of the Lord."** Isa. 2:12, Joel 1:15, 2: 1, 3: 14, Ezek. 13: 5, Malachi 4: 5, Acts 2: 20, IICor. 1: 14, I Thess. 5:2, II Pet. 3: 10. The term applies to the **"Day of the Lord's Return"** and includes both the Tribulation and the Millennium. The Christian Sabbath was never called the **"LORD'S DAY"** until after the book of Revelation was written and got its name from that source. It is called in the Gospel and the Epistles the **"First Day of the Week."**

THE "KEY" TO THE BOOK
OF REVELATION

The "Key" to this book is its "Three-Fold Division." Rev. 1: 19

1. The Things Which Thou Hast "SEEN."
2. The Things Which "ARE."
3. The Things Which "SHALL BE HEREAFTER."

This is the only book in the Bible where the Divisions are given,

And they are given here by Christ Himself.

When John wrote the book of Revelation in A. D. 95-96 the Christians were undergoing a persecution under the Roman Emperor Domitian, and as a result of this persecution, John had been banished to the Isle of Patmos, a small rocky island in the Aegean Sea, 30 miles off the west coast of Asia Minor, and opposite the city of Ephesus. John was Pastor of the Church at Ephesus at the time of his banishment, and it was to that Church that the first Message to the Seven Churches was Addressed. John was banished for "the word of God, and his testimony of Jesus Christ."

THE THINGS WHICH
THOU HAVE SEEN

The revelation of Jesus Christ, which God gave him to show his servants what, must soon take place. He made it known by sending His angel to His servant John, who testifies to everything he saw; that is the word of God and the testimony of Jesus Christ. Blessed is the one who reads the words of this prophecy, and blessed are those who hear it and take to heart what is written in it, for the time is near. Rev. 1:1-3(NIV.)

John the Apostle was transported to the future by the angel and given a vision on the Lord's Day, while on the Isle that was called Patmos, for the word of God, and for the testimony of Jesus Christ. Revelation 1: 10- 20 lets us know that John was in the Spirit on the Lords Day and he heard behind him a loud voice like a trumpet, which said: "Write on a scroll what you see and send it to the seven Churches: to Ephesus, Smyrna, Pergamum, Thyatira, Sardis, Philadelphia and Laodicea." Now John turned around to see the voice that is speaking to him and what he saw was seven golden lampstands, and among the lampstands was someone "like unto the Son of Man," dressed in a robe reaching down to his feet and with a golden sash around his chest…. His voice was like the sound of rushing waters. In his right hand he held seven stars, and out of his mouth came a sharp double –edge sword. His face was like the sun shining in all its brilliance. When John saw him, John fell at his feet as though he was dead. Then He placed his right hand on John and said: "Do not be afraid. I am the first and the last. I am the living one; I was dead, and behold I am alive for ever and ever! And I hold the keys to death and Hades." He continues by saying:

"Write, therefore, what you have seen, what is now and what will take place later. The mystery of the seven stars that you saw in my right hand and of the seven golden lampstands is this: The seven stars are the angels of the seven Churches, (Messengers or Preachers of the seven churches), and the seven lampstands (or candlesticks) which you saw are the seven Churches." And He goes on to give John messages for each of the seven churches. Revelation chapters 2 and 3 are the messages given to John for the seven Churches.

The Apostle John addresses the Churches as their brother and companion in tribulation. John was not talking about the "The Great Tribulation," for that is not for the Church but for Israel, and is still future. When John addresses the seven Churches of Asia Minor, they were going thru a heavy persecution under the Roman Emperor Domitian, and as a result, the Emperor had banished John to the Isle of Patmos, a small rocky island in the Aegean Sea, 30 miles off the west coast of Asia Minor, and opposite the City of Ephesus. John was the Pastor of the Church at Ephesus at the time of his banishment, and it was to that Church that the first messages to the seven Churches were addressed. John was banished to the Isle of Patmos for "the Word of God, and his testimony of Jesus Christ."

John lets us know that he was "in the Spirit on the Lord's Day." The meaning of the words "Lord's Day" is not clear in some areas. It's believe by some that the "First Day of the week" or the Christian Sabbath is meant, others believe that John Meant the "Day of the Lord." However, this term (Day of the Lord) applies to the "Day of the Lord's Return from Heaven" and includes both the Tribulation and the Millennium. However, the Christian Sabbath was not called the "**Lord's Day**" until **after** the book of Revelation was written and got its name from that source. It is called in the Gospels and the Epistles the "**First Day of the Week.**"

It is not likely that John was caught up as Paul was, into the Third Heaven and seen and heard that entire account he describes in the book of Revelation on <u>one</u> Sabbath Day, and as the book (Revelation) from chapter 5 is a description of the things that are to come to pass in the "**Day of the Lord**;" what better understanding of the "**Lords Day**" can we have than that John was projected by the Holy Spirit across the centuries into the "**Day of the Lord**" and had visualized to him the things that will come to pass in that day. I believe this to be the most likely solution of the question. For John then found himself in the "**Day of the Lord**."

In verse 17-18 of Chapter 1 of Revelation tells us that John heard behind him a great voice, as of a trumpet, which said "I am Alpha and Omega, the First and the Last," "I am He that liveth, and was dead; and behold, I **am ALIVE FOR EVERMORE, AMEN**; and I hold the keys to death and hades." This statement along identifies the speaker as the Lord Jesus Christ Himself. However, John had his back turned to the speaker, and when he turned around he saw one like unto the **SON OF MAN** standing in the midst of "Seven Candlesticks." (Lampstands may be a better translation.) A candlestick requires a light such as a candle, which is self-consuming, while a lampstand is for the support of a lamp whose wick instead of burning away is fed from the oil within. In the Scriptures oil is emblematic of the Holy Spirit, and as Jesus Himself interprets the "**Lampstands**" as meaning the seven Churches to whom He was about to send messages by John the Apostle, not as the light but simply the "**Light Holder.**" From the fact that Jesus speaks of stars and Lampstands it is clear that we are living in the night time of this Dispensation, for stars and lampstands belong to the night.

The Vision that John saw was that of the **GLORIFIED "SON OF MAN."**

When Jesus ascended into the Heavens; He took with Him His **Humanity,** and we now have in Heaven the man Jesus Christ. I Tim. 2:5. When Jesus was on earth he was as the "**Son of Man,**" a Prophet, Now as the Son of Man in Glory, He is a priest, and when He comes again it will be as the "**Son of Man**" to reign as **KING.**

While Jesus, during the time of John's vision, was and is now serving as High Priest in Heaven, until His return to Earth as "**KING OF KINGS.**" In John's vision, He was not seen engaged in any High Priestly work. However, He was clothed in a High Priestly robe, and He was not wearing a MITRE upon His head, or Kingly Crown. His description was more like that of a **JUDGE,** which also confirms the evidence that John was transported into the "Day of the Lord," and that Johns' vision of Christ is as Christ shall appear after His High Priestly work is finished and before He assumes His Kingly Office. This is still further and will be revealed as He appeared on the Mount of Transfiguration when "His **Face** did shine **AS THE SUN,**" Matt. 17:2. However, we read in Rev. 21:23 that "The inhabitants of the New Jerusalem will have no need of the sun or the moon to shine on it; for the glory of God gives it light, and the Lamb is its lamp. The Prophet Malachi tells us that when Jesus comes back, He will be the **Sun OF Righteousness** (Malachi 4: 2)

We now see that the Apostle John's vision of the son of man was as He shall appear at the second stage of His Return, the "Revelation." So we have in John's description of the person of the "**Glorified Son of Man**" circumstantial evidence that John saw his vision of the Son of Man, not on a Sabbath Day (or the Lord's Day as we now call it), but was projected by the Holy Spirit forward into the "**Day of the Lord**" and saw Him then as He appeared as the **Judge,** and the coming "**SUN OF RIGHTEOUSNESS.**"

"**THE THINGS WHICH THOU HAST SEEN**" IS THEREFORE THE VISION OF THE Son of Man in the mist of the "**seven lampstands.**" Rev. 1: 10- 20**.**

THE THINGS WHICH "ARE."

The Messages to the Seven Churches, Rev. 2: 1-3; 22. As these Messages were to seven Churches that were in existence in John's day, and to whom he personally wrote, there are those who believe the theory that John was in the Spirit on a certain Sabbath or "Lord's Day," and naturally they claim that John at that time could not have been transported into the "Day of the Lord." However, now we know that those Churches were **REPRESENTATIVE CHURCHES;** that would **become** defined periods in Church History, which would not be understood until the history of the Christian Church would be complete, and that will not be until the "Day of the Lord;" which means that John could have been projected in vision by the Spirit into the "Day of the Lord," and after his vision of the Glorified Son of Man, the messages to the "Seven Churches" were dictated to him by the Son of Man Himself, that John when he was returned to the Isle of Patmos could send them to the Churches. It is note-worthy that the "messages to the seven Churches" are inserted between two visions, the **"vision of Christ"** in the midst of the "Seven Lampstands" in Rev. 1: 12-17 and the **"Vision of the four and Twenty Elders"** round about the throne, in Rev. 4: 1-6.

As Revelation chapter four is a vision of the **"Glorified Church"** with the Lord, after the Church has been caught up (I Thess. 4: 13-17), then **"The Things Which Are"** which also includes Revelations two and three, must be a description or an outline of the "Spiritual History" of the Church from the time when John wrote the book of Revelation in A. D. 96 down to the taking out of the Church, otherwise there is no view of the Church during that period, for the Church disappears from the earth at the close of Rev. chapter three and was not seen again until she reappears with her Lord in Chapter nineteen. This explanation of the "Messages to the

Seven Churches" was hidden to the early Church, because time was required for Church History to develop and be written, so a comparison could be made to reveal correspondence pertaining to the messages. If it had been clearly revealed that the Seven Churches stood for "Seven Church Periods" that would have to elapse before Christ could come back, and there would have been no incentive to watch.

While the character of these Seven Churches is descriptive of the Church during seven periods of Church history, we must not forget that the condition of those Churches, as described, were their exact condition in John's day. So we see at the close of the First Century the enhancing of "False Doctrine" was at work in the Churches. The Churches are given in the order named, because the peculiar characteristic of that Church applied to the period of Church History to which it was assigned. It also must not be forgotten, that, which has a distinctive characteristic of each Church period, does not disappear <u>with</u> that period, but continues on down through the next period, until the end, thereby increasing the imperfection of the visible Church, until it ends in an open Apostasy.

THE FOLLOWING ARE MESSAGES WRITTEN TO EACH OF THE SEVEN CHURCHES:

I. THE CHURCH AT EPHESUS. (A BACKSLIDDEN CHURCH REV. 2: 1-7)

The complaint that Christ makes against this Church is that it "had left its First Love." Its character is seen in its name, for Ephesus means to "let go," or "to relax" It had become a **backslidden Church.** Paul the Apostle who founded it, warned it of what should happen, in his parting message. (Acts 20: 29, 30.) The significance of this warning is seen in Rev. 2: 6. Here Paul's "wolves" are called Nicolaitanes. They were not a sect, but a party in the Church who were trying to establish a "Priestly Order."(They are found today in some Churches.)

II. THE CHURCH AT SMYRNA. (A PERSECUTED CHURCH. REV. 2: 8-11)

Smyrna root meaning is "bitterness," and means "Myrrh," an ointment associated with death, and we see in the meaning of the word a prophecy of the persecution and death which was to befall the members of the Smyrna Church. They were told not to "fear" the things that they should be called on to suffer, but to be faithful "unto" death, not "until" death. Or, not until the end of their "natural" life. They were not to "recant" when called upon to face

9

a Martyr's death, but remain faithful until death relieved them of their suffering. Their reward would be a "Crown of Life." This is the Martyr's crown.

They were told that the "author" of their suffering would be the Devil, and its duration would be "ten days," which was probably a prophetic reference to the "Ten Great Persecutions" under the Roman Emperors, beginning with Nero, A.D. 64, and ending with Diocletian in A.D. 310. Seven of these "Great Persecutions" occurred during this "Smyrna Period" of Church History. However, it may refer to the 10 periods extended from A. D. 170 to Constantine A. D. 312

III. THE CHURCH AT PERGAMOS (A LICENTIOUS CHURCH REV. 2: 12-17.)

In this Message Pergamos is spoken of as "Satan's Seat." When Attalus III, the "Priest-King" of the Chaldean Hierarchy, fled before the conquering Persians came to Pergamos, and settled there, that's when Satan shifted his capital from Babylon to Pergamos. Satan has always felt that he was better than God; so at first he persecuted the followers of Christ, and at that time Antipas was one of the martyrs. But soon Satan changed his tactics and began to exalt the Church, and with the help of Constantine, united the Church and State, and offered all kind of inducements for worldly people to come into the Church. Constantine's motive was more political than religious. His intentions were to incooperate his Christian and Pagan subjects into one people, and in during so consolidate his Empire. The result of this union was that two false and harmful doctrines found their way into the Church and caused many uncontrollable problems. The first was the "Doctrine of Balaam," and the second was the "Doctrine of the Nicolaitanes," which has already been considered under the message to the Church at Ephesus. The Doctrine of the Nicolaitanes

Secured control in the Ephesus Church period that was seen in the first great Council of the Church held at Nicaea, in A.D. 325. The Council was composed of about 1500 delegates, however, the laymen outnumbered the Bishops 5to 1.

The story of Balaam in the book of Numbers Chapter 22 to 25 inclusive, gives us an exclusive picture of "Balaam's Doctrine." When the children of Israel on their way to Canaan had reached the land of Moab, Balak the King of Moab sent for Balaam the son of Beor, who lived at Pethor on the river Euphrates, to come and curse them for him. When the Lord would not permit Balaam to curse Israel, he suggested to Balak that he invite them to the feast of "Baal Peor," a sexually unrestrained party, having no regard for accepted rules or standards. And thus cause Israel to fall into a snare that would so anger the Lord that He would Himself destroy them. This Balak did, and the result was that when the men of Israel went to those sensual feasts and saw the "daughters of Moab" they committed fornication with them, which caused God to send a plague that destroyed 42,000 of them. Now the word "Pergamos" means "Marriage," so when the Church entered into a union with the State, it was guilty of "Spiritual Fornication" or "Balaamism."

At this time a sensuous form of worship was introduced into the church; the character of the preaching was changed, and most of the "Pagan Festivals" were adopted, to please the Pagan members of the Church, and attract more Pagans to the Church. The winter Solstice was believed to enter on the 21st day of December, which was believed to be the shortest day in the year, and it is not until the 25th that the days begins to lengthen, which was regarded throughout the Heathen world as the "birthday" of the "Sun-God," and was a high festival, which was celebrated at Rome by the "Great Games" of the Circus, Constantine was advised at that time to change the birthday of the Son of God, from April, (at which time He was probably born,) to December 25th, because as He was the "Son of Righteousness," what more appropriate birthday could He have than the birthday of the Pagan "Sun-God"?

It was at this time that the "Post-Millennial Views" had their origin. The Church had become rich and powerful, It was believed that by the union of Church and State, a condition of affairs would develop that would usher in the Millennium without the return of Christ. Since some scriptural support was needed for such a doctrine, they claimed that the Jews had been cast off **forever,** and that all the prophecies of Israel's future glory were intended for the Church only. This period extends from the accession of Constantine A.D. 312 to A.D. 606, when Boniface III was crowned "Universal Bishop."

IV. THE CHURCH AT THYATIRA. (A LAX CHURCH. REV. 2: 18-29)

In His commendation of this Church, Christ lays the emphasis on their "**works,**" as if they depended on them, and claimed their deserved merit for "works" of "Supererogation (during more than is expected)." But He had a complaint to make against them that was terrible in its awfulness. He charges them not merely with permitting a bad woman, Jezebel, who called herself a "Prophetess," to remain in the Church, but with permitting her to "teach" her pernicious doctrines, and to seduce the servants to commit fornication, and to eat things sacrificed to idols.

This woman was a "pretender," and called herself a "prophetess," who she was, is still questionable; no doubt she was of noble lineage. She certain was a woman of commanding influence. Whether her real name was Jezebel or not, she was very much like her prototype in the Old Testament, Jezebel the wife of King Ahab, she was not by birth a daughter of Abraham, but a princess of idolatrous Tyre, at a time when its royal family was famed for cruel savagery and intense devotion to Baal and Astarte. She was born into a family of "Takers," and "Deceivers." Her father was Eth-Baal, a priest of the latter deity, murdered the reigning monarch Phallus, in order to succeed him. And then Ahab, King of Israel, married Jezebel, in order to strengthen his Kingdom, and she, aided and abetted by King Ahab, introduced the licentious worship of Baal into Israel, and killed all the prophets of the Lord she could lay her hands on. And this influence she exercised, not only while her husband was alive, but also during the reign of her two sons; and her daughter married the son of Jehoshaphat, King of Judah, and introduced idolatrous worship into Judah. Jezebel's policy was so triumphant that there were only seven thousand people in Judah who had not bowed the knee to Baal, not kissed the hand of his image. In Revelation (2:20) she is used as a type of false teachers who, as the Church of Rome, developed, wedded Christian doctrine to pagan ceremonies, as Jezebel engulfed Israel in idolatry. (II King 9: 22) So Jezebel caused all Israel to sin after the sin of Jeroboam the son of Nebat. I King 16: 29-33. It is believed by many Biblical scholars even today, that the story of Jezebel and her licentious worship practice written in I King 16, is why many Churches will not except Woman Preachers and Pastor as being sent by God. A careful comparison of this "Message" with the Parable of "The Leaven" will reveal the correspondence between the two, the "Jezebel" of the Church of Thyatira, being the "woman" of the Parable, who inserted the "Leaven" of "False Doctrine" into the meat of the Gospel. This period extended from A. D. 606 to the Reformation A. D. 1520.

SERMON # 1

TEXT: Nehemiah 6: 3

SUBJECT: "We are doing a great work and we can't come down."

Introduction:

God created the world and all that is in it, therefore God is at home in the world. God goes from one tent site to another, from one home to another and from one dwelling place to another; so that the work that God calls us to do is with the people whom God seeks to call His own.

Let's take a look at Nehemiah's story, which could really be our story too. Sometime we are uneasy about our blessings and we began to wonder if we have given enough of ourselves to God, particularly when the blessings doesn't look like a blessing to us. And then the first thing we want to do to, relieve the uneasiness is to establish tributes to God; you know, beautifying our Sanctuaries, building larger Churches and having more Church programs. But such sacrifices are some of our efforts to please and appease God. Whether we are motivated by devotion or fear, we need to know that God's heart is given to and for the wefare of God's people. That's why when we are doing a great work; we ought not to come down. For Nehemiah is telling us in this text, that we should be too busy to be trifling; in other words, we should be doing a great work so that we can't come down. (yes) If we come down, the work will cease; if we come down, Satan will shift us like wheat; if we come down, the Lord will not build the house and I heard David say "Unless the Lord build the house, he that labored, labors in vain. () "I'M so glad I don't lean on my own understanding; but I lean on Christ. Nehemiah leaned on the Lord and the work didn' t cease; and he didn't come down. (yes) If we don't come down, we can do God's will in God's way, and in God's own time; if we don't come down, the devil won't have a chance to shift us like wheat, because James said, "If we resist the devil, he will flee from us." So stay on the wall "Church" you are doing a great work and you can't come down.

Body:

Here in our text, Nehemiah is working at finishing the walls of Jerusalem; and yet his enemies are still trying to bring trouble upon him. Tobiah and the other adversaries of the Jews was trying to use the wall build-up as an attempt to hinder their work; but Nehemiah, realasing that they were doing a great work and that his dependency was on the Lord, so he didn't stop to have a meeting with them; sometime we have a meeting about anything and everything, but they keap on working and the walls was finished in 52 days; and it's believed that they even rested on the Sabbaths days; and their enemies looked on them with wonder and there was no doubt in anybody's mind as to where their help came from. It came from the Lord. And if you are helped by God, Miraculous things happens. Abraham, was helped by God and he was provided with a ram in the bush; Moses, was helped by God, and the Red Sea opened up and they were able to walk across on dry land; Elisha, was helped by God, and fire rained down from Heaven to devour the sacrifice on the altar at Mt. Carmel and licked-up all the water in the trenches. It lets us know that when we are doing God's work, then we are doing great work and we must depend on God's blessings, for only God can really help us. For we are His audience. You see we need to know, who is on stage? The real question is who is the main attraction? Who is the subject of every song and every sermon? Who is the reason around whom we have gathered? Whose name is lifted to the voted ceiling and etched in every stain glass window? So you see not only are we God's audience, but when building a wall for the Lord or in other words when in worship or service for the Lord, we become God's audience, and we really don't need to pray for the Holy Ghost to show up, because if its God's work, He's already there.(yes) Nobody have to tell God how to be a good host. For when Adam and Eve were in the garden, God provided everything for them, so that in the cool of the eveing they could worship and commune with Him. However, they became disobedient, and there disobedience resulted in the necessity to serve and when we serve, we must remember to serve one another, for that's the lesson that Jesus left for us. So now we worship God in order to serve Him, we don't serve in order to worship. For worshipping is what happens when Heaven and Earth meet together. When men and women stretch their hands up to the Heavens and sing praises to the Lord; and the Lord comes down to meet them in the midst of it. For the scripture tells us that "Where two or three are gathered together in his name and on one accord, that He will be in the midst." And that's what worship is all about. "When Heaven meets Earth." "When the Spirit of God indwells the spirit of man," Then we should give God our best; simple because we love Him. Nehemiah's people did what they did cheerfully, because they love God, and when their enemies heard what they had done; The scripture said that "they were much Cast down…."

Sometime people with great aspirations are targeted by those who attempt little and achieve even less. Instead of rising to the level of great achievers, some people are content to live well below their abilities, pulling others down, instead of pushing them toward success. Underachievers would rather destroy than help them achieve success, because if they have a good example in front of them, they just might have to "reach for a star."

San Ballot and Tobiah tried to stop the rebuilding of the wall thru the elimination of its leader, Nehemiah. But when called to come down to their level; when called to come from God's work to engage in foolishness, Nehemiah refused to fall for their trap. But he left a message for us and for all ages to come; that in spite of our deceivers; in spite of our detractors; in spite of those who would like to see us fail; (I heard Him say) that "I am carrying on a great work and I can't come down." When others seek to divert your attention from excellence and achievement, in Church work; in academics; in family relations and professional work "busy work", () Let them know that you cannot be deflected from God's work; let them know that you are to busy to be trifling. God has given us a job to do, and we can't stop until that job is done. Nehemiah realized that the Christian experience is a race that we must run; and we must run it with patience, laying aside every weight and the sin that so easily besets it. If we are to win the prize, as Christians we are waging a war with the world, the flesh, and the devil, and we need the whole armor of God to prevent Satan from preventing us from fulfilling our jobs. We should not try to give God our spiritual junk food, for God don't deal with junk of any kind. We should worship Him in spirit and in truth.

Conclusion :

It was the Israelites worship experience that empowered God's dispossess, and gave them the strength to stay on the wall and not come down, that the work might not cease. And I say unto you today, worship the Lord with all of your heart and soul; Worship Him as though it was your last opportunity. For you may understand the physical and material use of building, (but I stop by to let you know) that except the Lord bless the building; it does no good for men to build. For if the model and design be laid in pride and vanity, or if the foundation be laid in oppression and injustice, God certainly does not build there. If you don't acknowledge God, then you have no reason to expect His blessings; and without His blessing all is nothing. That's why the Israelites sang the songs of degree in Psm. 121—134. Some folk call them pilgrim songs, because they were compose and sang by Jewish pilgrims journeying to

Jerusalem for the feast days. If you are building for the Lord, then you should be abl;e to join in with them. For they were some what like you and I. Coming from all over Palestine; we should be singing the Same songs ourselves. As they were coming from the villages and the Towns, coming from the east and the west, coming from the north and the south; from the plains of Sharon and Mt. Carmel; from Bethel and Shiloh from Jesrel and the salt Valley. They had been on the road a long time and now they can almost see the Holy City, want be long now. Every step brings them closer to the city of their highest Joy. Can't you hear them singing "I will lift **up** mine eyes unto the hills from which cometh my help." You see Jerusalem, the Holy City, geographically and theologically, is always **UP**. When I come to Church on Sunday morning, my Church might be on level ground geographically, but I'll be looking **UP**. "I will lift up mine eyes,"

For you can't see Jerusalem looking down; you can't see Jerusalem until you look up. If you look up, you should hear them singing the pilgrim songs; can you hear them? "I will lift up mine eyes;" Where does my help come from; The Lord who made Heaven and Earth;" can't you hear them singing; "they that trust in the Lord shall be as Mt. Zion; can't you hear them;" "If it had not been for the Lord on my side;" Can you hear them? "Except the Lord build the house, they labor in vain that build it! Except the Lord keep the City, the watchman worketh but in vain." And then when I come to the gate, those inside can't open the gate and He will have to let them know that I've done a great work and I havn't come down. You see, the gate represents security and refuse. And I can still hear them singing "Lift up your head, O ye gates; and be ye lifted up, ye everlasting doors, and the King of Glory shall come in" and He can open the gate. Now who is this King of Glory? (repeat) The Lord of Host; great and mighty! He is the King of Glory! He is the alpha and Omega! He is the Lily of the valley and the Bright and morning Star. Because the work didn't cease, He'll open the gate for you; because you gidn't come down, He'll open the gate for you and you will be able to hear Him say Well Done! Well Done! Well Done thou good and faithful servant………..

END END END

I. THE CHURCH AT SARDIS. (A DEAD CHURCH REV. 3: 1-6.)

The Church at Sardis was called a "Dead Church" though it had a name to live. That is, it was a "Formalistic Church," a Church given over to "formal" or "ritualistic" worship. This Church had the "Form of Godliness without the power." The word "Sardis" means "one who escapes" or those who "come out" and so it is a type of the Church of the Reformation Period. The reformation period was that period in the history of the Christian Church when Martin Luther and a number of other reformers protested against the false teaching, tyranny and claims of the Papal Church.

This Period began about A. D. 1500. The condition of affairs in the area dominated by the Papal Church continued to become undesirable, and brought about a crisis, when Martin Luther, on Oct. 31, 1517 A. D. nailed his 95 Theses on the door of the Church at Wittenberg, Germany. That date denotes the beginning of the Reformation period; (remember also that this Martin Luther, was not the Martin Luther of the 20th centure.) (later named in the United States as "The Lutheran Church Period.")However, the Reformation at Wittenberg, Germany was more a struggle for political liberty than a purely Christian or religious movement.

It had the advantage of encouraging and aiding the circulation of the Holy Scriptures that had up-to-now been a sealed book, the revival of the Doctrine of "Justification by Faith," and a reversion to more simple modes of worship. While that threw much light on the Word of God, it interfered greatly with the spiritual state of the Church, until it could actually be said truthfully, "**That the Church had a name to live and was dead.**" The "Sardis Period" extended from A. D. 1530 to about A. D. 1750.

SERMON: # 2.

TEXT : ACT 13: 1

Introduction:

It goes without question, that worship is the most central and significant aspect of the life and ministry of the Christian Church. All over the world, week after week, people gather to worship God in the person of Jesus Christ. People of various backgrounds, differencing in denominations and giving experience to an assortment of worship styles as declared by David unapologetically; when he said; "I will bless the Lord at all times; His praise will continually be in my mouth, O' magnify the Lord with me, let us exhorts his name together. If there is any one aspect of the Church that distinguishes her from other institution in our society; it is worship: For there is no possibility of the Church being the representative of Christ in the world, without **WORSHIP**.

Body

Worship is in its essence, the autobiographical sketch of a congregation,

Whom God has called to be His people in the world. As a matter of fact, worship is the area where the power of God, enables the Church to be "**The Church**". While worship cannot be defined in any absolute terms, I believe Franklin M. Stigler said it best, when he said "To worship is to quicken the congruence (or to bring on one accord) by the Holiness of God; to feed the mind with the truth of God; to purge the immigration by the beauty of God; and be able to open the

22

heart to the love of God and to devote our will to the purpose of God." You art to be able to see this; The reason we worship God is because we can't help it. I believe that Augustine said it best when he declared that "Thou have made us for thyself O' God; and our Souls are restless until we find our rest in thee." ()

Worship involves a devine offer and a human response; God offers himself in a personal relationship and the human family responses. God's love elitist our response in worship. The definition of the word "**Worship**" means one worthy of reverence and honor; when we worship we are declaring God's word. The Angle's sang "Worthy is the Lamb who was slain," and every creature answered "To him who sits upon the throne, and to the Lamb be blessings and honor and glory and might forever and ever." The four living creatures said "Amen". And the Elders fell down and worshipped. The Hebrew term "Cobor" which is also translated to mean "glory" means the honor or weight of God. The Greek term indicating worship in the New Testament is "pro-suit-ney-0;" meaning literally to kiss the hand toward one, or to prostate one's self before another in token of reverence. To speak of the content of worship is to speak of ministerial celebration, life, dialoged, giving an esh-kalogical fulfillment. When we peruse the Biblical records, we find consistence pictures of the significant and weightiest of worship. The sons of Adam, Cain and Abel worship God. Enoch lived in constant fellowship with God; Enoch walked with God; and he was **not**; for God took him. The Patriarchs, Abraham, Isaac and Jacob build Altars to God and worship the Lord. Under the leadership of Moses, Israel worship in celebration and proclamation of a covenant relationship established at Mt. Sinai.

We are reminded in the New Testament's gospel, that Jesus went to the Temple as were His custom; <u>and now</u> Christian worship should be an experience, not an act. It has to do with having an encounter; it is not entrainment, it is based upon an historical fact. The fact that God revealed himself **in history.** These historical facts are inclusive of God's creation, the incarnation, the works of Jesus Christ; His atoning death, His resurrection and His abiding presents in the life of believers. The way we think about these historical facts is called theology. Worship that is not grounded in the knowledge and love of God is not true worship. Theology that does not lead to the worship of God in Christ is false and dangerous. A sound theology serve as a corrective to worship, and true worship serves as the dynamic to theology. There is a model for worship, a pyridine that provides insight; an inspiration for the real purpose for worship in the life of the Church today. Isaiah gave us an autobiographical sketch of his calling when he declared "It was in the year that King Uzziah died, I saw also the Lord; seated on a throne, high and lifted up, and His train filled the Temple; and the Temple was filled with smoke and Isaiah cried out woe is me, for I am undone; I'm a man of unclean lips and I live among a people with unclean lips, and my eyes have seen the King, The Lord Almighty." Then one of the seraphs flew over to me with one of the tongs he had taken from the altar, with a hot coal on it, and touch my mouth and said "Your guilt is taken away and your sin is forgiven." And Isaiah heard the voice of the Lord saying whom shall I send? And who will go for us? And Isaiah said here am I, send me I'll go.

It was when Isaiah was at worship in the Temple, that he saw God in a new light, a way he had never understood God before. Isaiah saw God seated upon a royal throne, being attended by his Heavenly court. God was the one whose glory filled the whole earth. God's glory is the revelation of his attributes, which are manifested in himself and his creation. Therefore, worship has to do with revelation. Worship is always an opportunity to see God in new ways. Isaiah's vision seem to emphasize that God is both King and Judge, God is the one with absolute power and is altogether Holy. Later the Prophet Isaiah would speak of God as "The Holy-One of Israel." Worship demands that we look-up and catch a vision of

God. Perhaps some Churches are weak and ineffective in their ministry, because their God concept is off base, their picture and perception of God is marred.

You remember when God promised Abraham and Saraiah, that He would bless them with a son who would be known as Isiah; The Bible said they laugh. And God raised this Question to them, "is there anything too hard for God?' And like Abraham and Sariah; our problem in many cases are that our image, our concept of God, our perception of God is somewhat off base. We see a God who is limited; who is impotent; a God whom we want to make finite; a God whom we want to bring down and shape Him into own image. Many Christians and Church people today are spiritually impotent; they attend Church every Sunday and yet their lives remain dysfunctional; they are not able to handle the challenges of life; they live with no power; no anointing; no courage; no patience; no faith; no hope and no Love. Mainly because they fail to Look-up and see worship as an opportunity, to receive a revelation of God. Jerusalem might be on level ground but if you want to see the New Jerusalem, you have to look up. ()

Conclusion:

Our ancestors knew the value of looking-up in worship, and seeing God. They had a healthy God concept; they said speaking of God, that, "He was so high, you couldn't get over Him; so low, you count get under Him, So wide you couldn't get around Him (). They said speaking of God, "He may not come when you want Him to: but whenever He comes, He is always on time. When we look-up in worship, we position ourselves to be spiritually empowered by the image of God. Worship demands that we look-up and see ourselves in relationship to God. Whereas, Isaiah worshipped God and saw God in His holiness, he also saw himself; when Isaiah saw the holiness of God, he felt his own antiqueness and cried out in a confession of his own spiritual bankrupness. To see ourselves as we really are is not a pleasant experience; Dr. Gaylord Wilmore, one of the Civil Rights Leaders out of PA. on

Dr. M.L.K. Jr. staff; taught a class at N.Y.T.S. on Sanctification; & he said that "The closer I get to God; the farther away I see I am from God." It would do well for the moral majority and other religious groups who fill that they have reached some spiritual penal of perfection; that fill that live upstairs, while everybody else live downstairs. You see, worship demands that we take a look at ourselves; and in during so we would have to say like Paul "O' Richard man that I am;" for in worship if we look-up we would be able to see the Church as a hospital for the sick and not a hotel for the righteous; when we look-up we are reminded that we are saved by grace, kept by grace, and we are to heaven by grace. It's not of any goodness that we have to offer God, but rather, its God's grace extended to us. () () Grace; Grace is God giving us a 2nd chance.

I remember in the Church I pastored in N.Y., there was an older sister, that came up to me one afternoon and said "Pastor I never did get a chance to sin like other folk, because I was always in the Church; now I don't know if she was trying to fool <u>me</u> or to fool herself; because every person born of a woman, weather you were raised in the Church or on the street corner, everyone has sinned; everyone has missed the mark; everyone has come short of the glory of God; everyone like sheep has gone astray. However, we must not just see ourselves in profound abasement, with our depravity revealed by God's Holiness. We must also have a consciousness that our sins has been dealt with and the barrier that mars our relationship with God has been removed. For Isaiah's impurities' was removed under the figure of a cleansing by one of the Ser-a-phims with a hot coal. The hymn writer said it like this: "Amazing Grace how sweet the sound that saved a Retz like me……..". When we look-up, we are reminded that we are saved by Grace; kept by Grace, and we live by Grace; we also worship by Grace and we serve by Grace. By Grace we have a revelation of God; is there anyone out there, who knows my Lord? () () Do you know that He's worthy! ()……….(singing… Amazing Grace)…….

<u>END</u>

V. THE CHURCH AT PHILADELPHIA (A FAVORED CHURCH. REV. 3: 7-13.)

The meaning of the word Philadelphia is "Brotherly Love," and well describes the charity and brotherly fellowship that dissipated the bitter personal animosities that characterized the theological disputants of the "Sardis Period," and made possible the evangelistic and missionary labors of the past 150 years. There are three things said of the Church at Philadelphia; they are:

1. It had a "little strength." It was like a person coming back to life who was still very weak. It was the "dead" Sardis Church "revived," and Revivals have always been characteristic of the Philadelphia Period. These Revivals began with George Whitefield in A. D. 1739, followed by John Wesley, Charles G. Finney and D. L. Moody.

1. It had set before it an "open door," that no man could shut. Note that this promise was made by "**HIM**" (The risen Christ), who "hath the key of David," He that 'openeth' and no man shutteth; and 'shutteth' and no man 'openeth.'

2. It was to be kept from the **"Hour of Temptation"** (Tribulation), that shall come upon **ALL THE WORLD,** and as there has never as yet been a **worldwide** Tribulation, this "Hour of Tribulation" must still be future and refers to the **"GREAT TRIBULATION"** that is to come upon the "whole world," just before the return of the Lord to set up His Millennial Kingdom, and as the promise is that the "Philadelphia Church" shall not pass through the Tribulation, then this appears to be additional proof that the Church shall be "caught out" **before the Tribulation.** The Philadelphia period covers the time between A. D. 1750 and A.D. 2000 +, for only God knows the when. We must never forget that the

characteristics of all these periods continue on in the Church down to the end. However, they are now more mechanical and based on business methods, and there is less spiritual power, and this will continue until Christ returns.

I. THE CHURCH AT LAODICEA.(A LUKEWARM CHURCH. REV. 3: 14-22)

Christ has nothing good to say about this Church, but much to complain of. He says "I know thou work, that thou art neither hot nor cold: I would that thou were cold or hot. So because you are lukewarm, neither hot nor cold; I am about to spit you out of my mouth. There is nothing more disgusting or nauseating than lukewarm water. So there is nothing more repugnant to Christ than a lukewarm Church. It was that "chilly spiritual atmosphere" of the Church of England that drove John Wesley to start those outside meetings which became so noted for their "outburst of spirituality," and it was the same "chilly spiritual atmosphere" of the Methodist Church that drove William Booth into becoming a "Red-hot" Salvationist. Now Salvation has always been freely offered to who-so-ever will; but is conditioned upon repentance and faith in Jesus Christ (John 3:16; Heb. 2: 3). It proceeds from the love of God, and is based upon the atonement given by Christ, and is realized in forgiveness, regeneration, sanctification, and culminates in the glorification of all true believers.

Our Churches today are largely in this "lukewarm" condition. There is very little of warm-hearted spirituality. There is much going on in them, but it is largely mechanical and of a social character. Societies, clubs and committees are in great numbers, but there is an absence of "spiritual heat." The cause of this "Luke- warmness" in the Church of Laodicea was **Self-Deception.** (See Rev. 3: 17-19) They thought that they were rich, and outwardly they were, but Christ saw the poverty of their heart. Remember, the Laodiceian period is still going on and will be until the Church is taken out or Jesus returns. We still have many such Churches in the world today.

There are more so, than any other period in the history of the Church. If we were to visit some of these Churches today, they would take pride in showing us the building, they would praise the preaching and singing, they would boast of the character of their congregation, the exclusiveness of their membership, and the attractiveness of all their services, but if we suggested a series of meetings for the "betterment of the **Spiritual Life,**" or the "conversion of the unsaved," they would say—"Oh, no, we do not want such meetings, we have need of nothing." The Church at Laodicea was not burdened with debt, but it **was** burdened with **WEALTH.**

The Laodiceian condition describes the spiritual Luke warmness and worldliness which will prevail in the professing Church of Christ at the end of the Laodiceian period. It will show what it considers spiritual; Rich, cultured, religious ritualistic; this Church will have become as self-satisfied and worldly as to have ostracized Christ completely. Since Jesus is represented prophetically as standing on the outside knocking for admission to come in; (Rev. 3: 20). How is Christ to get back into His Church? Does it require the unanimous vote or invitation of the membership? No. "If any men hear my voice, and open the door, I will come in to him, and will sup with him, and he with Me." Therefore, the way to revive a lukewarm Church is for the individual members to open their hearts and let Christ **re-enter, and in during so opens the door** for Christ's reappearance.

The character of the Church today is found in the Laodiceian period, and as the Laodiceian period is to continue until the Church of the "New-Born" is taken out, we cannot expect any great changes until the Lord Jesus Christ returns to earth. These "Messages to the Churches" clearly teaches the **decline of the Church.** That the professing Church instead of increasing in spiritual and world converting power will become and is now **"CLEARLY"** becoming lukewarm, faithless, and **CHRISTLESS.**

In Paul's Parable of the "Two Olive Trees" (Rom. 11: 15-27), he shows how the "natural branches" of the "Good Olive Tree," (Israel) were broken off because of **unbelief**, that the "wild olive tree" of the Church might be "grafted in," which in turn, because of unbelief, would be displaced that the **"Natural branches"** might be grafted again, showing that the Church does not take the place of Israel permanently, but simply fills up the "Gap" between Israel's "casting off" and "restoration to Divine favor." As the Laodiceian period closes the "Church Age," the Church disappears at the end of Rev. Chapter three, and Israel comes again into view. These "Messages to the Churches" clearly teach the **Decline of the Church.** They teach that the professing Church instead of increasing in spiritual and world converting power will become lukewarm, faithless, and CHRISTLESS.

In Paul's parable of the "two Olive trees" (Rom. 11:15-27), he shows how the "**natural branches**" of the "**Good Olive Tree,**" (Israel) were broken off because of unbelief, that the "Wild Olive Tree" of the Church might be **"grafted in,"** which in turn, because of **Unbelief,**

Would be displaced that the "**Natural branches**" might be "**grafted back again."**

SERMON # 3.

Subject: "An Open Door Policy"

Text: Revelation 3: 7-8

INTRODUCTION:

We want to start this message off with the next to the last Church of Asia Minor, the Church of Philadelphia. Now I know that when I speak of the word "Philadelphia," many of you think of a city in Pennsylvania. However, I'M talking about a city twenty-five miles south of Sardis, in Asia Minor. The word literally means "love of a brother," now you will hear in the first part of the word, an English word, "filial," that is love of a child for a parent. "Philadelphia."

BODY:

There is no question about the meaning of the word "Philadelphia." It means "Brotherly Love, and describes the charity and brotherly fellowship that dissipated the bitter personal animosities that characterized the theological disputants of that period and made possible the evangelistic and missionary labors of the past 200 + years. There were many rumors about this Church and three of them were as such:

1. It had been said that it had a "little strength." It was like a person coming back to life, who was still very weak. It was the dead "dead" Sardis Church revived, and revivals have been very characteristic of this period.

2. It had set before it an "open door," that no man could shut. Now that THIS PROMISE WAS MADE BY Him who has the "Key of David," He that openeth and no man shutteth; and shutteth and no man openeth. It has been said that in 1793 He open the doors in India, and since, then the Lord open the doors into China, Japan, Korea, Africa and the inlands of the sea, until there is not a Country in the whole world where Missionary cannot go.

3. It is to be kept from the "Hour of Temptation" or (Tribulation,) that shall come upon all the world, and as of yet, there has never been a **worldwide tribulation,** so this **"Hour of Tribulation"** must still be future and refers to the **"Great Tribulation"** that is to come upon the "whole world," just before the return of the Lord Jesus to set up His Millennial Kingdom, and since He promise the "Church of Philadelphia" that they shall not pass thru the Tribulation, this is additional proof that they shall be caught-up before the Tribulation! The Philadelphia period covers the time between A. D. 1750 and A. D. 200 +. This period will remain in effect until Christ return. The Churches are now more mechanical and based on business methods now, and therefore, has less spiritual power, (yes) you don't see anybody being raised from the dead anymore; or anybody walking on water anymore, **"but it's not over yet!"** This period will continue until Christ returns. And when Christ returns; the scripture say's when Christ returns, **those that died in Christ shall rise first, and those left behind shall be caught-up to meet Him in the air; there to be with the Lord forever and ever....** I stop by to let you know today, that it's not over yet, there is still an "Open door policy"; our text tells us that "He knows our works," and He has the key of David, He can open it and no man can Shute it; and He can

Shute it and no man can open it. And I heard Him say "I will keep thee from the hour of tribulation." **YES,** if you confess with your mouth, and believe with your heart, **Yesss** thou shall be saved! "God has Open the Door for you to come thru." (For the Spirit said unto John "that the tribulation would come upon the entire world to try them that dwell upon the earth. Can you hear the Lord saying to John behold, I come quickly; come on in, we have an open door policy, hold that fast which thou hast, that no man take thou crown. God has an open door policy! He that has an ear let him hear what the Spirit saith unto the Churches. "Well, I stop by to let you know, **that we are the Church,"** and one day He picked me up, turn me around...... and I can feel Him moving right now......! (YESSS)!

Can you hear Him? Can you feel Him? You art to know that there is nothing more repugnant to Christ than a Luke-Warm Church. I don't know about you, but I don't want to be spud out of His mouth. Christ has promised us that "He will stand at the door and knock; and if any man hear His voice and open the door, He says I will come in to him and will sup with him, and he with me. Jesus lets us know that "To him that over cometh, will I grant to sit with me in my THRONE" (YESS YESS)

We have too many of our Churches today that are largely in this "Luke-warm" condition. And as such, there is very little of warm-hearted spirituality. There is a whole lot going on in the Church today, but it's largely mechanical and of a social character. We have committees, societies, and clubs are multiplied, but there is an absence of "Spiritual Heat." Revival meetings are held, but instead of waiting on the Lord for power, high priced Evangelists and musicians are hired, and soul winning is made a business, just as the Church of Laodicea found itself in self-deception. They thought they were rich, and outwardly they were, but Christ saw the poverty of their heart. There are many such Churches in the world today. More so than other period in the history of the Church; Many of these Churches have large building with stained glass windows, eloquent preachers, with large congregations and large salaries and are well endowed. The Church at Laodicea was not burdened with debt, but it was burdened with wealth.

The trouble with the Church today is that it thinks that nothing can be done without money and that if we only have the money, the world could be converted in this generation. But I heard the Lord say that the world is not to be converted by money, but by the spirit of God. The Church today is still living in the Laodiceian period. They are poor, though they appear to be rich; but not only that, they are also blind; or to put it more accurately "**Near-Sighted.**" But they possessed no medicine that would restore impaired Spiritual vision, for only God can do that.

There was a startling revelation made to the Church of Laodicea, and is being made to us today. Christ said "**Behold, I stand at the door and knock.**" Now listen; these words are generally quoted as an appeal to sinners, but not this time; this time they are addressed to the Church, and to a Church in whose midst Christ had once stood, but now found Himself excluded and standing outside knocking for admittance. (Ask yourself, is Christ standing outside of your Church today?) And don't look at that as though it doesn't happen. Christ was excluded from his on Church in His day, **for they rejected Him;** excluded from the world, **for it crucified Him;** excluded from his Church, for He stands outside its doors now **Knocking for Entrance.**

Now the question is, how did Christ come to be outside of the Church anyway? He had been within it once or there never would have been a Church. So how did He come to leave? It's also clear that they did not throw Him out, for they do not seem to have missed His presence. They continue worshiping Him, singing His praises, and engaging in all manner of Christian Services, yet He had withdrawn. Why? The reason is summed up in one word---worldliness. Some Churches try to bring the world into the Church; but we are to be in the world but not of the world, for God did not leave us here to travel this road along. I heard Him say "I'll be with you always, even until the end of the world." I tell you. That we are His Church, and He has an open door policy (yess) (if anyone will, let him come!)

So, the real question is, how is Christ to get back into His Church? Does it require the unanimous vote or invitation of the membership? No, No, I hope not. I heard Him say; "If any man hear my voice, and open the door, I will come into him and will sup with him, and he with me." So the way to revive a lukewarm Church is for the individual members to open their hearts and let Christ re-enter, and I believe the door will open for His reappearance.

Now Paul in Romans 11: 15-27, talks about an olive tree. Now the olive tree is wild by nature; and if a branch is broken off that olive tree, and falls to the ground and begin to share in the nourishing sap from that olive tree root, well, we know that that the branch does not support the root; the root supports the branch; and I stop by to let you know, that we too are the branches. Let me tell you something; Israel through that "GOD" was for them and them only, but because of unbelief, some of their branches were broken off of the olive tree, but if they did not persist in their unbelief, they were grafted back into a good olive tree.

Now watch out! Remember; that those branches were broken off because they didn't obey God, and those of us who obey and believe in Him are grafted in because we do believe in Him. () () (Anybody here believe in God? I don't know about you, but I believe in Him.) So you art to be humble and grateful and careful. For if God did not spare the branches He put there in the first place, don't you know, that He won't spare you either. God can be hard on them, who disobey Him, but I stop by to let you know that He's very good to you when you continue to love and trust Him. That's why He keeps an "Open door policy." Paul says in Roman 8:14, "that if we live by the Spirit, we live to the Lord; and if we die, we die to the Lord." So, weather we live or die, we belong to the Lord. For God have concluded that all have sin and fallen short of the mark, that He might have mercy on all. (Aren't you glad about it?) (I don't know about you, but I'm glad that one day He grafted me back into the olive tree; had mercy on me; picked me up, turn me around..............().

As we close: The last three verses of Roman 11 ask a question;

Who has known the mind of the Lord? Or who has been His counselor? Who has given to God that God should repay him?

For of Him, and through him, and to Him are all things: to whom be Glory forever. Amen. () ()

If we hold on to God's unchanging hands, and live by his command () () He'll make it alright, REPEAT! "I KNOW HE'S ALRIGHT"

END END END

III. THE THINGS WHICH SHALL BE AFTER THESE THINGS.

We have now come to the Third Division of the Book. The Three Divisions of the Book do not overlap nor are they concurrent. The word translated "hereafter," permits a "time space," while the words "after these things" refer to the things that shall immediately follow the completion of the "Church Age," as prefigured in the Messages to the Seven Churches. The Church disappears from view with the close of the third chapter of Rev. and is not heard of again until the nineteenth chapter of Rev., where her marriage to the Lamb is announced. Rev. 19:7-9. The removal of the Church at the end of the third chapter opens the way for God to renew His dealings with Israel and take up the broken thread of Jewish History. That the portion of the Book from chapter three to the end of chapter nineteen is largely made up of symbols taken from the Old Testament, such as the Tabernacle, Ark of the Covenant, Altar, Censer, Elders, Cherubim, Seals, Trumpets, Plagues, etc., is conclusive evidence that we are back on Jewish ground, and that the Parenthetical Dispensation of the Church is complete, and that the last or "Seventieth Week" of Daniel's "Seventy Weeks" is about to be fulfilled. It is clear therefore that if we are to find an explanation of the symbols of Daniel's "Seventy Weeks" we must look to the Old Testament, for these symbols.

However, Chapters four and five are introductory and preparatory to the "Prophetic Action" of the: Seals," "Trumpets" and "Vials," and must be considered first.

1. THE HEAVENLY DOOR. (REV. 4: 1.)

The scene now changes from earth (Isle of Patmos) to Heaven John tells us that, **After This,** (after his vision of Christ in the midst of the "Seven Candlesticks," and his foreview of the history of the Christian Church, which carried him down to the end of the Church Age, he looked, and behold a door was open in Heaven, and the same voice that spoke to him from the midst of the "Seven Golden Candlesticks," which was the voice of Christ (Rev. 1: 10-13), and with the clearness and sweetness of a trumpet said "**COME UP HITHER AND I WILL SHOW THEE THINGS WHICH MUST COME AFT+ER THESE.**" And John adds "**Immediately I was in the spirit:** and, behold, a throne was set in Heaven, and ONE sat on the Throne."

The experience of John was some-what like the experience of the Apostle Paul, when he was caught up into Paradise. He was not sure whether he was in the body or out of the body, the Apostle Paul was uncertain (2.Cor. 12: 2-4.) However, John said that he was in the Spirit at once. The difference between them was that, while Paul was forbidden to speak, John was told to "**write in a book**" of the things he had seen and heard, and send them to the seven Churches of Asia. John's "Rapture" is a type of the **RAPTURE OF THE CHURCH,** and it is at this place in the book that the "**RAPTURE**" of the Church takes place. (Remember; this is a type of the rapture, at this time the rapture is still future.)

After the confession of Peter at Caesarea Philippi, that Jesus was the Christ, the son of the living God (Matt. 16: 13-28), and Jesus said "upon this rock of peter's confession that He would build His Church," He then said to His Disciples, "Verily I say unto you, there be some standing here which shall not taste of death, till they see the son of man **coming in His Kingdom**." And in the next chapter we read that "Jesus after six days takes' Peter, James and John his brother, and brings them up into a high mountain, (The mount of transfiguration) and was **TRANSFIGGURED BEFORE THEM.**" Matt. 17:

1-9. This scene was a type of the second coming of Christ, Moses being the type of the "resurrected Saints," and Elijah of the "Translated Saints."

Jesus had promised His disciples that some of them should not "taste of death" until they had at the very least, seen a vision of a rehearsal of the manner of His Second Coming, and this was fulfilled in this "Transfiguration Scene," therefore, the statement made to Peter and also to John, "If I will that he **"TARRY TILL I COME"** (John 21: 20-23), is fulfilled in John being caught up in vision and beholding, **before his death,** what he would have witnessed and experienced if his life had been prolonged until Jesus came back. Therefore John was permitted to live, until, **in vision**, he saw the return of the Lord. The Apostle Paul writes in I Thessalonians. "For the Lord Himself shall descend from Heaven with a SHOUT, with the voice of the ARCHANGEL, and with the trump of GOD; and the dead in Christ shall rise first: then we **which are alive** and **remain** shall be caught up together with them in the clouds, to meet the Lord in the air: and so shall we ever be with the Lord." (I Thess. 4: 16-17) John's taking up tends to corresponds with Paul's writing in Thessalonians. He was summoned by the "**VOICE OF CHRIST,**" and it will be the "**SHOUT OF CHRIST**" that shall summoned the saints at the Rapture. To confirm that the Church was "**CAUGHT OUT**" at this time and place; for we have in the description of the Throne, the statement that the Holy Spirit in His full and complete power is BACK IN HEAVEN. In none of the Epistles is the Holy Spirit invoked along with the Father and the Son, except in II Cor. 13: 14 because He is viewed there as abiding on the earth with the Church, convicting of sin, comforting believers, and gathering out the elect, but here He is no longer on the earth, but back in Heaven, and before the throne. And when the Holy Spirit goes back to Heaven, I Thess. 4:17 tell us that He will take the Church back with Him. And the presence of the Holy Spirit in Heaven is complete evidence that the events that follows are to take place after the Church has been "Caught Out," and therefore the Church is not to pass thru the Tribulation.

2. THE HEAVENLY THRONE. (REV. 4: 2-3, 5-6.)

The first thing John saw in Heaven was a **THRONE.** The Throne was not vacant, but **One** sat upon it, whom to look upon was like looking at glistening gems. The occupant of the Throne was God Himself. John in describing the New Jerusalem says, that its light is the "Glory of God." A light like unto a stone most precious, even like a JASPER stone, clear as crystal. John says in I John 1: 5 that God is light, and in him is no darkness at all. So that corresponds to John's heavenly view. However, Ezekiel 1:26-28 describes the "Glory of God" as the appearance of a sapphire stone: and upon the likeness as the appearance of a man above upon it. And he saw as it were the appearance of fire, and it had brightness round about. As the appearance of the bow that is in the cloud in the day of rain, so was the appearance of the "Glory of God." Now there are two things in Ezekiel's vision that correspond with John's vision of the "Throne of God." First that the form of the one who sat on the Throne could not be clearly distinguished, but that it was **RESPLENDENT WITH LIGHT** (to shine brightly)**:** And secondly, that there was a **RAINBOW ROUND ABOUT THE THRONE.** The person of God then, as He sits upon His Throne, is veiled in a Glory that can only be compared to the shining of some beautiful gem. But the real beauty of the Throne of God is, that it is surrounded by a "**RAINBOW**" that is emerald in color.

God used the rainbow as a covenant that He would not destroy the earth again by a flood. But that rainbow was **SEMI-CIRCULAR**, such as what we see in the heavens after the rain; but the **RAINBOW** Ezekiel and John saw around the throne of God was **CIRCULAR**. In this world we only see half a rainbow, or the half of things, in Heaven we shall see the whole of things. The rainbow is the sign of a covenant based on an accepted sacrifice, the sacrifice of Noah (Gen. 8:

20-22), and the rainbow about the Throne of God is the sign of a covenant based on the accepted Sacrifice of Christ on the Cross. The difference between Noah's Rainbow and the one around the Throne of God is, that Noah's is composed of the seven primary colors, red, orange, yellow, green, blue, indigo and violet, while the one around the Throne of God is EMERALD. Now what is the significance of the **"Circular Green Rainbow"** around the Throne of God? It simply means that God is a covenant keeping God, that His promises as to this earth shall be fulfilled. God will redeem the earth and bless it, until its hills, and valleys, and plains, shall teem with the green verdure, fruitful orchards, and bountiful vineyards of the long Millennial Day that is to follow those judgments.

This "Throne" was not the "Throne of Grace" for out of it proceeded lightings and thundering's and voices, that remind us of Mt. Sinai, and proclaim it to be the "**Throne of Judgment.**" Before, the Throne was a "**Sea of glass.**" This "Sea of Glass" was unoccupied, but later is seen mixed with **fire** (Rev. 15: 2-3), and occupied by martyrs of the tribulation period who get the victory over the **Beast,** and who have harps, and sing the songs of **Moses and the Lamb.** This "Glassy Sea" reminds us of the "Brazen Sea" that stood before Solomon's Temple (I Kings 7: 23-45), and thus was in front of the Ark of the Covenant, the "Mercy Seat" of which, was the earthly throne of God in Old Testament days.

This is a good time to remember that the earthly Tabernacle erected by Moses, with all of its vessels and instruments of service and mode of worship, was patterned after the "Heavenly Tabernacle." (Heb. 9: 23). Once we have knowledge of Moses Tabernacle and its various parts and vessels of service, then that should help us to understand John's Vision of the "Heavenly Tabernacle." Like John, Paul was "caught up" into Heaven, and saw the "Heavenly Tabernacle," and he clearly makes a comparison between it and the "Mosaic Tabernacle" in his letter to the Hebrews. The Throne that John saw in Heaven corresponds with the "Mercy Seat" of the Ark of the Covenant.

If the throne section of the Heavenly Tabernacle corresponds with the "most Holy Place" of the "Mosaic Tabernacle," and the "Four and Twenty Elders" section with the "Altar of Incense" and "Seven Lamps of Fire" corresponds with the "Holy Place," then the "Sea of Glass" and the "Altar" should correspond with the "Court" of the Tabernacle. Hopefully this will help us to locate what John saw in the Heavenly Tabernacle. It is also instructive to compare the "Heavenly" and "Earthly" Tabernacles with the "Tabernacle of Man." For here the Spirit part of man corresponds to the "Most Holy Place" of the Tabernacle, the "Soul" part to the "Holy Place" and the "Body" part to the "Outer Court." Since the only entrance from the "Holy Place," into the "Most Holy Place" of the tabernacle was through the "Veil." So the only entrance from the "Soul Part" of man into the "Spirit" part is through the "Gate of the Will." And it is only when the "Will" part of man, surrenders to the Holy Spirit that God will take up His abode in the "Spirit" part of man, as He took up His residence in the "Most Holy Place" of the Tabernacle on the "Mercy Seat," and man became a regenerated soul.

3. THE FOUR AND TWENTY ELDERS

Rev. 4:4 speaks of twenty four seats round about the Throne and sitting upon the seats were twenty four Elders, clothed in white raiment; and they had on their heads **Crowns of Gold.** Now these Elders were representatives of **redeemed mankind.** For the name Elder is never applied to angels, beside, angels don't have **"crowns"** and they don't sit on **"thrones."** These Elders then must be representatives of the Old and New Testament Saints that have been redeemed by the **Blood of Christ**. Take a look at their position; they are seated on **"thrones,"** not ordinary seats, they remind us of Daniel's Vision of the **"Judgment Seat OF Christ"** Dan. 7: 9-10 while the "Thrones" were placed (ready for those who should be found worthy to occupy them) they were as yet unoccupied. Now as the "Thrones" that John saw were occupied by **Crowned** Elders. Then those Elders must have passed the "fiery test" of the judgment of Reward (II Cor. 5: 10, I Cor. 3: 11-15), and received their crowns. ("The Incorruptible Crown." I Cor. 9:25-27. "The Crown of Life" Rev. 2: 10. "The Crown of Glory." I Pet. 5: 2-4. The "Crown of Righteousness." II Tim. 4: 8. The "Crown of Rejoicing." I Thess. 2: 19- 20. These Elders were given a new song to sing; for Rev. 5: 9- 10 say's "And they sung a **New Song,** saying, thou art worthy to take the book and to open the seals thereof, for thou wast slain, and hast **REDEEMED US TO GOD BY THY BLOOD,** out of every kindred, and tongue, and people, and nation; and hast made us unto our God Kings and PRIESTS; and we shall reign on the earth."

Now this could not be said of angels, or any other created heavenly beings, for they have not been redeemed by the blood of the Lamb, nor are they to be "Kings" and "Priests" on the earth.

Now these Elders are sitting on Thrones and are wearing Crowns, they are not dressed in royal robes but in "white raiment," the garment of a Priest. They are the members of a "ROYAL PRIESTHOOD." I Pet. 2: 9. The time has not yet come for these Saints to reign, for they are engaged in Priestly duties, having "Golden Vials full of odors, which are the **prayers of saints,**" in their hands. Rev. 5: 8.

The word "**Elder**" in the majority of places where it is used in the scriptures means the representative head of a city, family, tribe or nation, so the "Four and Twenty Elders" are representative of the redeemed human race. Now Twenty Four is the number of the Priestly Courses or Movements, as given in I Chron. 24: 1-19. When David distributed the Priests into "Courses" he found there were **24 Heads** of the Priestly families, and these 24 Heads he made representative of the **WHOLE PRIESTHOOD.** As the Elders are representative of both the Old and New Testament Saints, and the Old Testament Saints are represented by the Twelve Tribes of Israel, and the New Testament Saints by the Twelve Apostles of the

Lamb, they together make up 24 representative characters. In the description of the New Jerusalem, the 12 foundation stones are named after the Twelve Apostles of the Lamb, and the 12 Gates after the Twelve Tribes of Israel. Rev. 21: 10-14. While the Twenty Four Elders are representative of the Old and New Testament Saints, they do not, as a whole, represent the Church, for the Church is composed only of New Testament Saints. The fact that the New Testament Saints, as represented by the Twelve Apostles, are required to make up the 24 representative characters (Elders), is evidence that the Rapture of the Church takes place before the Tribulation.

4. THE FOUR BEASTS (REV. 4: 6-11) OR(LIVING CREATURES)

The "Four Living Creatures" are not in the same class with the "Elders," for they have no "thrones" or "crowns" or "harps" or "golden vials." They are the "Guardians" of the Throne of God, and accompany it wherever it goes. Ez. 1:24-28. They are four in number, which is the earth number, and therefore have something to do with the earth. That is, they are interested in the "**re-genesis**" of the earth to its former glory before the fall. They have eyes before and behind and within, which reveals their intelligence and spiritual insight of things past, present and to come, and they are tireless in their service, for they rest not day nor night, saying, "**Holy, Holy, Lord God Almighty, which was and is, and is to come.**" The word here used means a "living being" or "creature," while the word used in chapters 11, 13, and 17, means a wild untamed animal.

The first time these "Living Creatures" are mentioned in the Bible is in Gen. 3: 24, where they are called "CHERUBIM," but are not described. They were placed at the entrance of the "Garden of Eden" to prevent the re-entrance of Adam and Eve, and to keep the way of the "Tree of Life." It would appear as if at the place where they were stationed there was a place of worship to which Cain and Abel resorted to make their offering, and that it was from there that Cain went out from the "PRESENCE OF THE LORD." Gen. 4: 16.

The dissimilarity between Ezekiel's "Living Creatures," and John's "Living Creatures" can only be explained on the supposition that there are different orders of "Living Creatures" or "Cherubim," each adapted to the service he is created to perform. In Isaiah's Vision in the Temple of the Lord seated on His Throne, He saw a Heavenly order of beings that he called the "Seraphim." They had six wings, like John's "Living Creatures," and cried "Holy, Holy, Holy, is the Lord of hosts: the whole earth is full of His Glory" (Isa. 6: 1-4), but they stood above the throne, while Ezekiel's Cherubim supported the Throne, and John's "Living Creatures" were in the midst or around the Throne. Whatever significances there may be in the different forms the "Cherubim" or "Living Creatures" took, it seems clear to me, that they do not represent the Church, They appear to be attendants or officials attached to the Throne of God, for Rev. 6:1-8 lets us know that they summon the four Horsemen to appear, and in Rev. 15: 7 one of them hands to the "Seven Vial Angels," the "Golden Vials" filled with the wrath of God. They were seen in Rev. 4: 9-11 giving glory and honor and thanks to Him that sits upon the Throne, who liveth forever and ever, the "Twenty and four Elders" Then falls down before Him that sits upon the Throne, and worship Him . . . and cast their crowns before the Throne, saying, "Thou art worthy, O Lord, to receive glory and honor and power: for Thou hast created all things, and for thy pleasure they are and were created."

5. THE SEVEN-SEALED BOOK. (REV. 5: 1-14).

Now, what is this "SEVEN SEALED BOOK"? Writing to the Ephesians, Paul said in Eph. 1: 13-14 "Ye were **SEALED** with the Holy Spirit of promise, which is the earnest of our inheritance until the **redemption** of the **PURCHASED POSSESSION**." Therefore, there must be a possession that is to be redeemed. Paul tells us in Rom. 8: 22-23. "We know that the whole creation groaneth and travaileth in pain together until now. And not only they, but ourselves also, which have the "First fruits of the Spirit," even we ourselves groan within ourselves, waiting for the adoption, to wit, the redemption of our body." (This is believed to take place at the first resurrection).

We now know that there were something lost to mankind and the earth that is to be redeemed. It is the inheritance of earth and of immortal life given to Adam and Eve that was lost in the fall of Eden. When Adam sinned he lost his inheritance of the earth, and it passed out of his hands into the possession of Satan, to the disinheritance of all of Adam's seed. The forfeited Title Deed is now in God's hands and is awaiting redemption. Its redemption means the legal repossession of all that Adam lost by the fall. Adam was powerless to redeem the lost possession, but the law provides in Lev. 25: 23-34 that a kinsman may redeem a lost possession. That Kinsman has now been provided in the person of **JESUS CHRIST**; who was born of the Virgin Mary; lived and died on an old rugged cross that we may have the right to the tree of life. To become a kinsman He had to be born into the human race. This the Virgin Birth accomplished. However, Jesus paid the **REDEMPTIVE PRICE,** which was His own **BLOOD**, on the cross, but He has not as yet claimed that which He then purchased. When the time comes for the redemption of the **PURCHASED POSSESSION** Jesus will do so. That time and the act will be shown in the description we are now using. The **"SEVEN SEALED BOOK"** is the "TITLE DEED" to the redeemed inheritance. In the Old Testament, when a kinsman desired to redeem a property, he took his position, in the gate of the City and brought ten Elders as witnesses, to advertise his purpose. In Ruth 4: 1-12; this practice is illustrated in the story of Boas and Ruth.

When the "strong angel" proclaimed with a loud voice; "Who is worthy to open the Book, and to lose the seals thereof?" That was the notice designed to attract public attention and the "Kinsman Redeemer" to appear. But John tells us that there was no (redeemed man) in the Heaven, nor in Earth, neither under the Earth, who was able to open the Book, neither to look thereon. When John saw that there was no "MAN" worthy to open the Book, he wept. John wept because he knew what this BOOK was, and that if there was no one to open this "BOOK" (for this Book) was "THE BOOK OF REDEMPTION", and that all hope of the redemption of the Earth and of man was gone. But John's sorrow didn't last very long, for one of the ELDERS said-"Weep not: behold, the LION OF THE TRIBE OF JUDAH, the ROOT OF DAVID, hath prevailed to open the Book, and to lose the 'seven Seals' thereof." And John saw a LAMB, as it had been slain, that he had not notice before, and it was standing in the midst of the Throne, and of the "Four living Creatures." John had not seen the Lamb before, because it had been seated on the Throne with the Father, and came out of the Glory of the Throne, when the Elder begin to speak.

John looked for a "LION" and saw a LAMB. But the Elder was right in calling it a "Lion," for Jesus was about to assume His Title as the LION OF THE TRIBE OF JUDA, and reign with KINGLY POWER. The lion is the king of beasts. Of Judah it is predicted, in Gen. 49: 8-12, that His seed would hold the scepter, and become King of Israel as "Shiloh," and rule the world. Mary, the mother of Jesus, was of the tribe of Judah (LK. 3:33). When we compare Rev. 5: 7 with Dan. 7: 13-14, the two visions are identical; Rev. 5: 7 adds to that which was hidden from Daniel, that the Kings and priests of the Church Age are to be associated with the Son of Man (seen here as "a Lamb as it had been slain") when He "shall reign on the earth." Now we know that the Lamb was not an animal, because Rev. Verse 7 says "And HE (THE Lamb) came and took the Book out of the right hand of HIM that sat upon the Throne." This may very possible be the sublimest individual act recorded in the Scriptures; for the redemption of the whole creation of God depends upon it. It is still future and will only take place after the Church has been "CAUGHT UP" and Judged, and before the tribulation period begins, and we that have been redeemed by the blood of the Lamb, will witness the scene, and take part in the "song of Redemption" that follows. Rev. 5: 8-10.

When the LAMB leaves the Throne to take the Book, His Mediatorial word ceases, and His work as "Kinsman Redeemer" begins as soon as He is handed "THE BOOK," which is the "TITLE DEED" to the Purchased Possession, He and only He has the right to break its Seals, and claim the "Inheritance," and DISPOSSESS the present tenant SATAN. This He will proceed to do, as He breaks the SEALS. However, Satan is not evicted right away, Satan contests the claim and it is only after a prolonged conflict that he is finally dispossessed and cast into the lake of fire.

The manner of redemption of a lost inheritance is presented in the Old Testament. A property could not be alienated from the original owner or his heirs for a longer period than 50 years, at which time it reverted back to the original owner. If however for some reason the owner was forced to sell it, it could be redeemed by the next of Kin on the payment of the proportionate amount of its value due until the next "Year of Jubilee."(50 years Lev. 25: 8-17). (See redeeming method Ruth 4: 1-12, & Jer. 32: 6-12).

Daniel's Seventieth Week (Dan. 9: 1-27)

As the events recorded in Rev. 6: 1 to Rev. 19: 21, are connected with the last, or Seventieth Week of Daniel's **"Seventy Weeks,"** it is necessary that we stop here and explain what is meant by Daniel's **"Seventieth Week."**

In B. C. 538 the Prophet Daniel had been in Babylon for 68 years; and by a study of the Prophecy of Jeremiah (Jer. 25: 11), he discovered that the "Seventy Years" Captivity of his people was nearing its end, and so he set his face unto the Lord, to seek by prayer and supplication to know the exact time of its ending, and while he was praying the angel

Gabriel appeared to enlighten him. In Dan. 9:20-23 Daniel was concerned about the expiration of the "Seventy Years" of the Captivity, and the restoration of his people to Palestine, and the rebuilding of the City of Jerusalem and of the Temple. However, the angel Gabriel came to disclose to him something more important than that. He made known to Daniel that, that would not end the troubles of Israel. That while the Jews would return to Jerusalem at the end of the "Seventy Years" of Captivity that another period must elapse before the Kingdom would be restored to them, a period of **"SEVENTY WEEKS."**

"**SEVENTY WEEKS**" are determined upon thy people (Daniel's people the Jews) and upon the Holy City (Jerusalem), to finish the transgression, and to make an end of sins, and to make reconciliation for iniquity, and to bring in everlasting righteousness, and to seal up the vision and prophecy, and to anoint the most Holy. Now these Seventy weeks are divided into three periods. One of seven weeks, one of sixty two weeks, and one of one week. Now it took 49 years to rebuild the Walls of Jerusalem, which was done in the first period of 7 weeks. So now we have a key to this mystery. By dividing 7 weeks into 49 years, we find that 1 week is equal to 7 years. Now let's combine the first period of 7 weeks with the 2nd. Period of 62 weeks and we get 69 weeks; then if we multiply the 69 weeks by the 7 years, and then combine them into years, we'll have 475 years. Now History will show us that the 1st period where the walls of Jerusalem was rebuild, begin in B.C. 445. Now this period ended when Jesus rode triumphal into Jerusalem in A.D, 30. Now the Jewish calendars used in the scriptures had only 360 days per year, unlike our calendars which has 365 ¼ days per year. Therefore the period between B.C. 445 & A.D. 30 is 483 years of 360 days per year. There was no break between the first and second period, thus 69 weeks of Daniel's 70 weeks ended with Jesus ride into Jerusalem in A.D. 30. However, there are still some prophecy's that have not been fulfilled, therefore the Last week must still be future.

Dan. 9:27 tells us that the antichrist shall make a covenant with the Jews for one week and in the middle of the week, he would break the covenant. Now because Jesus promise the Church in John 14 that He was coming back to receive them unto Himself, there was a time space between the 2nd and 3rd period that was hidden, so that the Church would not fail to watch. Know therefore and understand, that from the going forth of the commandment to **restore and to build Jerusalem** unto the '**MESSIAH THE PRINCE'** shall be SEVEN weeks, and THREESCORE AND TWO WEEKS: The street shall be built again, and the wall, even in troublous times. And after THREESCORE AND TWO WEEKS shall MESSIAH BE CUT OFF, but not for Himself: and the people (Roman) of the **PRINCE THAT SHALL COME (Antichrist)** shall destroy the City and the Sanctuary; and the end thereof shall be with a flood, and unto the end of the war, desolations are determined. And he (Antichrist) shall confirm the covenant with many for **ONE WEEK** (the last of Daniel's seventieth week): And in the mist of the week he (Antichrist) shall cause the Sacrifice and the ceremony to cease, and for the **overspreading of abominations** (Abomination of Desolation spoken of by Christ in Matt. 24: 15) he shall make desolate, even until the **consummation,** and that determined shall be poured upon **the desolate.** (Dan. 9: 24-27). Therefore, the ascension of Christ brought in **THE CHURCH AGE OR THE DISPENSATION OF GRACE.** So we are now living in the last half of the last week of Daniels 70 weeks. Not only that, but we are living in the night time of these last days, and when morning comes; there is going to be a shout from Heaven, and **Jesus** will come riding on a cloud, the dead in Christ will rise first and those still alive will be caught-up to meet Him in the air.

Weeping may endure for a moment, but Joy come's in the morning.

THE SEVEN SEALS OPENED

FIRST SEAL (REV. 6: 1-2)
(A White Horse)

When the **LAMB** broke the "First Seal," the first or "lion-like living creature" cried with a voice like of thunder; "**COME.**" The command "TO COME" was to the rider of the white horse. When he appeared, John says; and I saw, and behold a WHITE HORSE; and he that sat on him had a bow; and a crown was given unto him: and he went forth conquering, and to conquer.

Who is the "Rider" upon this white horse? He is not Christ, as some claim, for Christ as the Lamb, is holding the "**Seven Sealed Book**" and breaking its "Seals." Christ does not appear as a white horse rider until Chapter 19: 11-16, when He comes with the armies of Heaven to engage in the battle of Armageddon. Then He is called "Faithful and True," and on His head there will be many "Royal Crowns," and He is clothed in a vesture dipped in Blood, and His name is called the "**WORD OF GOD,**" and there is no weapon of warfare in His hand, but a sharp sword comes out of His mouth, and the effect upon His enemies will be swift and terrible.

This "Rider" has a "bow," no arrow is mentioned, and he is not crowned at first, but the "Victor's Crown" will be given to him later, as a reward for his victories which are prolonged and bloodless. This is the picture of a brilliant, strategically, and irresistible conqueror, whose victories will dazzle the world, and elevate him to a leadership that will place him at the head of the Ten Federated Kingdoms of the revived Roman Empire. Somewhat, like Napoleon Ist he will rise from the ranks until a crown will be given him. His triumphs will be due to his skillful diplomacy. He will come in peaceably and obtain the Kingdom by flatteries. (Dan. 11: 21). As the "tool of Satan" he will be endowed with wonder working powers, and when he comes, he will find the world ready to receive him, for God will send upon its inhabitants a "**strong delusion**" that they will believe "**THE LIE,**" for that is what he will be. II Thess. 2: 9-11. For this White Horse Rider is the **ANTICHRIST**. He is the "PRINCE WHO IS TO COME" of Daniel's Vision of the "Seventy Weeks," and who will confirm the Covenant for "ONE WEEK," the last or "Seventieth Weeks," with Daniel's people the Jews. Dan. 9: 27.

This Covenant will no doubt, give them the privilege to return to Palestine and rebuild the Temple and re-establish their sacrificial form of worship, and national existence, in exchange for the financial assistance of the Jewish banker of the world in his schemes of establishing worldwide commerce, and the formation of a gigantic corporation, with its commercial center in the rebuilt city of Babylon, so that no one can buy or sell unless they have his "**MARK,**" (the "Mark of the Beast," Rev. 13: 16-17), for we are told in Dan. 8: 23-25, that he will cause astounding devastation and will succeed in whatever he does. He will destroy the mighty men and the holy people. He will cause deceit to prosper, and he will consider himself superior…. Yet he will be destroyed, but not by human power.

The rise of this White Horse Rider necessarily comes before the beginning of the "Seventieth Week," or the "**Seven Years**" of his reign, for he must have reach a position of power to make a covenant with the Jews at the beginning of the week, but he does not become "**THE BEAST**" as described in chapter 13: 1-8, until the middle of the week, After Satan has been cast out of Heaven and incarnates himself in him. His rise to power and the rebuilding of Babylon will take time, so the rapture of the Church will no doubt come before the beginning of the WEEK by some years. However, the establishment of the Antichrist's power will be comparatively peaceful, that peace will be short-lived as is evident from the breaking of the "Second Seal."

This "White Horse Rider" will be Satan's "**SUPERMAN.**" The Scriptures clearly teaches that a human being will someday arise to be the embodiment of all satanic power. He will be known as the "**WILFUL KING**" because he shall do according to his own will. He will be the Czar of Czars. He will have no respect for sacred things or places. He will cause a throne to be erect in the Most Holy Place of a Temple that the Jews will build at Jerusalem, and seating himself on it, he will proclaim himself to be God, and men will be commanded to worship him; and Satan will give unto him his power and his seat and great authority. (Rev. 13:1-10)

SECOND- SEAL (REV. 6: 3-4)
(A Red Horse.)

When it was broken John heard the second, or "Calf-like Living Creature" say, "Come," and a "RED Horse" appeared and went forth, whose rider was given a "**GREAT SWORD,**" and who had power to take peace from the earth, and cause men to kill one another. The symbolism is very clear. **Red,** the color of the horse, is a symbol of **Blood,** and the sword is a symbol of **WAR.** The time is clearly that prophesied by Christ ---"And ye shall hear of wars and rumors of wars... for nations shall rise against nations, and Kingdoms against Kingdoms." (Matt. 24: 6-7) This is a fulfillment of 1. Thess. 5: 3. "When they shall say PEACE AND SAFETY; then sudden destruction cometh upon them, as travail upon a woman with child; and they shall not escape." We should learn from this "**Seal**" that wars are likely to break out at any time and that there will be no lasting peace on earth until the return of the "Prince of Peace."

THIRD SEAL. (REV. 6: 5-6)
(A Black Horse.)

When the "**THIRD SEAL**" was broken, John heard the third or "Man-like Living Creature" say—"**Come,**" and a "**BLACK HORSE**" appeared and went forth, whose Rider held in his hand a "pair of balances," and John heard the voice of an invisible person in the midst of the "Four Living Creatures" say---"A measure of wheat for a penny, and three measures of barley for a penny, and see thou hurt not the oil and the wine." The BLACK HORSE signifies famine, and the Rider the **"Conserver of Food."** When all able bodied men are drafted for war, and no one left to sow and harvest the crops, then famine is sure to follow. So great will be the famine, that it will take a day's wages, to buy a two pints of wheat, (the daily ration of a slave.) What is meant by not hurting the **oil** and **wine,** may be, that as the olive tree and grapevine do not bear their fruit until some months after the wheat and barley harvest, and grow without much attention, their crops would not be so much affected by war, and therefore the Olive trees and grapevines were not to be ruthlessly destroyed by invaders for they were needed for medicinal purposes.

FOURTH SEAL (REV. 6: 7-8.)

(A Pale Horse.)

When the "FOURTH SEAL" was broken, John heard the fourth, or the "Eagle-like Living Creature" say---**"Come,"** and a **PALE HORSE"** appeared and went forth. The rider upon the pale horse is called **"DEATH,"** and that "HADES,**"** THE **"GRAVE,"** not **"HELL,"** follows after death like a great "Voracious Monster" to swallow up the victims of **"DEATH."** Here however the rider is personified and called **"DEATH,"** and his consort is called **"HADES,"** they are inseparable companions. The reference here is to some great **pestilence** that shall come upon the earth. After a devastating war, followed by famine, during which the dead are left unburied, therefore, a pestilence is sure to follow. The pestilence will sweep over a fourth part of the earth and it will probably be that part of the Eastern Hemisphere covered by the revived Roman Empire. It is believed that the destruction of human life will be so great in the days of the **"Fourth Seal"** that **HADES** will have to enlarge herself and open her mouth without measure, as foretold in Isa. 5: 13-16. However, the Church will not be a part of this judgement, having been "**caught out**" before as promised. But awful as those days will be, they will be only the **"Beginning of sorrows"** for those who are left. (Matt. 24: 6-8). Instead of the people repenting and calling on God, they will call upon the mountains and rocks to hide them from the face of Him that Sited on the Throne. Rev. 6: 15-17.

FIFTH SEAL (REV. 6: 9-11)
Sacrificial Altar
(The Souls of Martyrs.)

When the Lamb had opened the "**FIFTH SEAL,**" John saw under the "Sacrificial Altar," the "**SOULS**" of them that were slain for the "Word of God" and for the "Testimony they held." The fact that their "**Souls**" were under the "Sacrificial Altar" is proof that they had been offered as a "Sacrifice," therefore, they were **martyrs.** But they were not the Martyrs of the Christian Church, for the Martyrs of the Christian Church had been resurrected and taken up with the Church. But these Martyrs are those who "**will be**" Killed for the **"Word of God"** and their testimony, after the Church is caught out.

According to Christ in (Matt. 24: 9-14), a persecution will be brought about by the preaching of the "**GOSPEL OF THE KINGDOM.**" When the Church is caught out, the preaching of the "**GOSPEL OF THE GRACE OF GOD**" (Acts 20:24), which is being preached now, will cease, and the preaching of the "**GOSPEL OF THE KINGDOM**" will be revived. You remember the Gospel that John the Baptist preached, don't you? He preached "Repent ye: for the Kingdom of Heaven is at hand." Matt. 3:1-2. And as Malachi 4: 5-6 states, that Elijah the Prophet when he returns will preach also. It will be preached in all the world for a witness that the end of this dispensation is close to the end. It will also be preached by the Jews, and will be the announcement that Christ is on his way back to set up His Earthly Kingdom, and rule over the affairs of men. The Kings of the Earth will find this distasteful, particularly to

Antichrist and the Kings of the Ten Federated Kingdoms, and the outcome will be a "Great persecution" of those who preach and accept such a Gospel; now the **"SOULS"** that John saw under the "Sacrificial Altar," are the souls of those who shall perish that time of persecution. Sense there is no such thing as "Soul Sleep," and that disembodied Souls are conscious and can speak and cry, because John saw and heard these Souls cry with a loud voice-"How long, O Lord, Holy and True, dost thou not judge and avenge our BLOOD on them that dwell on the earth?" The character of their cry is even more proof that they are not the Martyrs of the Christian Church, for they would not cry to be avenged, but would say as Stephen said, "Lord, lay not this sin to their charge." Acts 7: 60, but there cry indicates that these Martyrs whose Souls are seen are mainly **JEWS**. This is still more likely when we consider that the "Gospel of the Kingdom" is to be preached to the Nations, and we know that Israel has never been numbered among the Nations. Num. 23: 9.

These Martyred SOULS were comforted, and told that they should rest for a "little season," about 3 ½ years, until their fellow servants also, and their brethren (the Jews) that should be killed, as they were, should be fulfilled. This promise is fulfilled in Rev. 20: 4-6. These are the Saints of the Most High that Daniel foresaw would receive the Kingdom. Dan. 7: 27.

SIXTH SEAL (REV. 6: 12-17)
(Physical changes.)

When the "SIXTH SEAL" WAS BROKEN, John tells us that there was a "GREAT EARTHQUAKE," and the "SUN BECAME BLACK AS SACKCLOTH OF HAIR," and the "MOON BECAME AS BLOOD," and the "STARS OF HEAVEN FELL TO THE EARTH," and the "HEAVEN DEPARTED AS A SCROLL," and "EVERY MOUNTAIN AND ISLAND WERE MOVED OUT OF THEIR PLACE. "These are great physical convulsions that shall shake the earth, and some of these great convulsions have happen before.

They were foretold by the Prophets of the old testament and by Christ Himself. We must never forget the "GREAT DARKNESS" that for 3 days overspread Egypt in the days before the Exodus (EX. 10: 21-23), and please don't forget the "DARKNESS" that settled over Jerusalem and Calvary on the day of the Crucifixion of Christ. (Matt. 27: 45).

The Prophet Zachariah speaks of a day that shall not be "LIGHT" or "DARK," and he associates it with an earthquake at the time of the return of the Lord. (Zach. 14: 1-7). On May 19, 1780, there was in New England what is called in history the "Dark Day." This is believed to be the fulfillment of Zach. 14: 1-7. It was not an eclipse of the sun, and yet it was dark enough to make the stars visible, and the chickens went to roost. The cause of that darkness has never been explained. Joel says in his prophecy that- "I will shew wonders in the heavens, and in the earth, blood, and fire, and pillars of smoke. The sun shall be TURNED INTO DARKNESS, and the moon into BLOOD, before THE GREAT AND TERRIBLE DAY OF THE LORD COME." (Joel 2: 30-31).

Isa. 13: 9-10 tells us that "the DAY OF THE LORD cometh, both with wrath and fierce anger, to lay the land desolate, and He shall destroy the sinners thereof out of it. For the stars of heaven and the constellations there of shall not give their light, the sun shall be darkened in its going forth, and the moon shall cause it's light not to shine." Now when we look at Isa. 34: 4 we read—"All the host of heaven (the stars) shall be dissolved and the heavens shall be rolled together as a scroll: and all their host shall fall down, as the leaf falleth from the vine, and as falling figs from the figtree." This corresponds to the "stars of heaven" of this "**Six Seal**", and not the constellations and heavenly bodies stars, for they are too far away to be affected by judgements on the earth, but to our own atmosphere, and to "**meteors**" and "**shooting stars,**" similar to the "Shooting stars" of November 13th, 1833, when they fell for three hours during the evening, and terrified the people so much, that they though that the world was coming to an end. Now these physical convulsions will be the earth's "TRAVAIL PAINS" as it labors to bring forth the NEW CREATION of the millennial age. Christ refers to this period in Matt. 24: 29, where He says—"In those days shall the Sun BE DARKENED (as it's light being obscured), and the MOON SHALL NOT GIVE IT'S LIGHT, and the STARS SHALL FALL FROM THE HEAVEN, (the principalities and powers of the Heavenly Places (EPH. 6: 12), not the powers and Kingdoms of the earth), Shall be SHAKEN." All these PHYSICAL CHANGES and CONVULSIONS will cause a great fear to fall upon all classes and conditions of men (7 classes are named (see Rev. 6: 15)). So these classes and changes will see the "HAND OF THE ALMIGHTY" in all of it. To them the "DAY OF JUDGEMENT" will become a reality, and in their fear and terror they will hide themselves in the dens and in the rocks of the mountains, and say to them **"FALL ON US, AND HIDE US FROM THE FACE OF HIM THAT SITTETH ON THE THRONE, AND FROM THE WRATH OF THE LAMB; FOR THE GREAT DAY OF HIS WRATH IS COME, AND WHO SHALL BE ABLE TO STAND?"** What a prayer? Instead of repenting and crying for Salvation, they will call on the mountians and the rocks to bury them from the sight of the almighty.

THE INTERVAL BETWEEN THE SIXTH AND SEVENTH SEALS

1. THE SEALING OF THE 144,000. (REV. 7: 1-8)

Here we have a short suppenson in the breaking of the **"SEALS"** that God's **"elect of Israel"** may be **"SEALED."** As God reserved 7000 in the days of Ahab who did not bow there knee to Baal (1. Kings 19: 18), so there will be a remnant according to the election of grace (Rom. 11: 4-6), and God will reserve 144,000 of Israels people who durning the period of the tribulation will not bow their knee to Antichrist. Now this **SEALING** is not the sealing of the Holy Spirit, that Eph. 1: 13-14 gives to the Believers; it is a "Sealing" at the hands of angels, spoken of in Matt. 24: 31. Rev. 14: 1, tells us that the **"FATHER'S NAME"** is to be written on their foreheads. We know that the followers of Antichrist will be "Sealed" in their foreheads or on their right hand, with the "Mark of the BEAST" WHICH IS THE NUMBER OF HIS NAME, OR 666. The "BELIEVERS" were "Sealed" on their foreheads, because their was no secret discipleship in God and everyone could see the **"SEAL."** (read Rev. 13: 16-18)

The 144,000, (12,000 from each of Israels original 12 tribes), will be of the earthly Israel, the "TRUE ACTUAL SEED" of Abraham, that are living at that time, and not of a mystical or spiritual Israel. Realizing that the **"TWELVE TRIBE"** were lost long ago among the nations; nevertheless, their whereabouts is not unknown to GOD. God knows where they are, and **who is who**, and in that day the angels, with omniscient precision, will seal them according to their tribe, 12,000 from each tribe. The Angel who has charge of the **SEALING** comes from the EAST. This is significant; It shows the characteristic of the **"Sealed Ones"** having their gaze directed toward the "SUN-RISING," as if looking for the fulfilment of the promise in Malachi, "Unto you that fear my name shall the 'SUN OF RIGHTEOUSNESS' arise with healing in His wings." Mal. 4: 2. The "Elect" then of Israel will be those who "fear Christ's name," and who, like as Simon and Anna watched for His First Coming, will be looking for the coming of their Messiah.

There is a difference in the names of the Tribes as here recored and the names of the original Twelve Tribes. Here the name of Dan and Ephraim are omitted, and the name of Joseph and Levi are substituted. The reason being that in Deu. 29: 18-21, we read that the man, or woman, or family, or tribe, that should introduce idoltry into Israel, should have their or its name **"blotted out"** from under heaven, and be separated out of the Tribes of Israel; for this is what the Tribes of Dan and Ephraim were guilty of when they permitted Jeroboam to set up **"Golden calves"** to be worshipped, one at Dan in the tribe of Dan, and the other at Bethel in the "Tribe of Ephraim." (1. King 12: 25-30.) And since the Tribes of Dan and Ephraim are in the list of the twelve Tribes that shall occupy the Holy Land during the Millennium (Ez. 48: 1-7, 23-29), It appears that the SEALING of the Tribes at this time is more for an HEAVENLY PRESERVATION, than to keep them for an earthly inheritance, and this is confirmed by the fact that they are later seen with the Lamb on the Heavenly Mount Zion. (Rev. 14: 1-5.) The fact that their names is not on this list of these "SEALED ONES" is to show that the Tribes of Dan and Ephraim must pass through the Great Tribulation unprotected by **Sealing.**

2. THE BLOOD WASHED MULTITUDE. (REV. 7: 9-17)

This "Blood Washed Multitude" introduces us to another class of the saved of the "End-time." They do not represent the Church, for the Church has already been taken out. They are different from the Elders, who represent the Church, for they **stand,** and have "**palms**" in their hands, while the Elders have **"crowns,"** and **"Sit on thrones,"** and have **"harps,"** & **"golden vials"** in their hands. They are an "elect body" of Gentiles gathered out from all nations, and kindreds, and people, and tongues. The statement that they "came out of Great Tribulation" does not necessarily imply that it was **"THE Great Tribulation"** that they came out of**, for that covers only the "last half"** of the week**,** and they are seen by John in the middle of the **"first half"** "of the week. But it simply states that they came out of "**great tribulation,"** and as the whole week is a period of tribulation, they could come out of tribulation any time durning the week. They are in reality, a vast multitude saved by the preaching of the "GOSPEL of the KINGDOM." While the Holy Spirit went back with the Church to escort the "Bride to be" home, it does not follow that He remained there. For in Old Testament times, and during the earthly ministry of Jesus, He was active in the conversion of men, and so it will be after the Church is caught out, He will remain active. Those who are converted during the Tribulation period, their conversion will be by the Holy Spirit.

It has been said that this "BLOOD WASHED MULTITUDE" is representative of the Gentiles who shall pass saftly through "The Great Tribulation," and who shall cry out "SALVATION" because they have been saved from death during the Tribulation and they shall serve God day and night in the new "Millennial Temple" on the earth for there is no day or night or Temple in Heaven. Now this is true of the Holy City, New Jerusalem (Rev. 21: 22-25), it is not true of Heaven, for they are not the same. The New Jerusalem is the place (City) that Jesus went to prepare for His bride, the Church (John 14: 2), and John declares that he saw it coming down **"out of"** Heaven. Rev. 21: 2. Therefore the New Jerusalem is not Heaven. However, that there is a **"TEMPLE" in Heaven** we are told in Rev. chapters 11: 19, 15: 5-8, and 16: 1. And the statement "That they shall hunger no more, neither thirst any more; neither shall the sun light on them, nor any heat, for the **Lamb** which is in the **MIDST OF THE THRONE** shall feed them, and shall lead them unto living **fountains of waters: and God** shall wipe away all tears from their eyes," is not Millennial but Heavenly in character. And further more this "Blood Washed multitude, **being Gentiles,** could not serve in an earthly **Jewist Temple."**

The Angelic Hosts was so thrilled and rejoicing at the sight of this "Blood Washed Multitude" that they will fall upon their face and worship God, saying, "AMEN: BLESSING AND GLORY, AND WISDOM, AND THANKSGIVING, AND HONOR, AND POWER, AND MIGHT, BE UNTO OUR GOD FOR EVER AND EVER. AMEN."

THE SEVENTH SEAL

(Silence) Rev. 8: 1

We must not forget that the number seven is considered the perfect number in Biblical history; and that the **"Seventh Seal"** Includes all that happens during the sounding of the **"Trumpets,"** and the pouring out of the **"Vials,"** and thus extends down to the ushering in of the Millennium. A good example would be an rocket fired into the air, then bursts into SEVEN stars, and one of these stars bursts into "Seven other stars. etc." and one of the second group of stars into a third group of "seven stars." So that the "Seventh" Seal includes the Seven Trumpets, and the "Seventh" Trumpet includes the "Seven Vials."

The "SILENCE" that followed the breaking of the "Seventh Seal" was preparatory to what was to follow during the sounding of the "Trumpets," and the pouring out of the "Vials." This **"SILEENCE"** was something remarkable, for there was nothing heard for a half hour. The four and Twenty Elders ceased their harp-playing; the angels hushed their voices, and the cherubrim and Seraphim and all the host of Heaven were silent; and so great was the **silence** that all Heaven was "AWED" by it; and John added that it lasted for **"HALF AN HOUR."** The suspense of the half hour of silence in "HEAVEN" was truly intense. But why that half hour of SILENCE? What was its intention? It was a period of silent preparation for the awful judgments that were to burst forth in the earth under the "Trumpets" and "Vials."

THE GOLDEN CENSER

(Golden Altar) Rev. 8: 2-5

Following the SILENCE in Heaven, John saw "SEVEN ANGELS" of official importance, for their positions was to stand in the presence of God, to whom "SEVEN TRUMPETS" would be given. Now Trumpets are used to call to war, to worship, for the convocation of the people, to proclaim Festivals, as the year of Jubilee, the Feast of Tabernacles, and for Judgments. Ex. 19: 16. Amos 3: 6. Joshua 6: 13-16. Zeph. 1: 14-16. These "Seven Angels" prepared themselves by taking the Trumpets that was handed them and took up their positions where they could in turn sound their Trumpets. But before the Trumpets were sounded John saw another Angel with a "**GOLDEN CENSER**" in his hand come and stand before the "Golden Incense Altar." The name of this "Angel Priest" is not given, some claim it was Christ, because he is our "Great High Priest," We are also told that He was given much incense, and that He offered with it the prayers of the "**ALL SAINTS.**" These were the Saints of the Tribulation period, and their prayers were for deliverance from their enemies. This will explain the remarkable act of the "Angel Priest" of filling the Censer with **FIRE FROM OFF THE ALTAR**, and casting it on to the earth, the effect of it was seen in the **VOICES** and **THUNDERINGS**, that broke the **SILENCE** of Heaven, and the **LIGHTINGS** and **EARTHQUAKE** on the Earth. As the same things happen when the "Seventh Trumpet" sounds (Rev. 11: 19), It appears that the "seventh Vial", the "Seventh Trumpet", and the "Seventh Seal," all end alike, and they all end at the same time, the "end of the week." The Judgments that follow on the earth as the Trumpets sound, and the Vials are poured out, are the answers to the prayers of the Saints for vengeance on their enemies.

THE SEVEN TRUMPETS

FIRST TRUMPET
(HAIL- FIRE- BLOOD) Rev. 8: 6-7.

This is the fulfillment 0f Joel 2: 30-31, where the Lord will repeate the **"PLAGUES OF EGYPT."** The exactness of these Judgements gives us the "KEY" to the exactness in the book of Revelation. At least 5 of the 9 **plagues of Egypt** are to be repeated during the Tribulation Period. The difference between these Egyptian Plague, and the Plague of the first Trumpet, is that the situation will be reversed. The Children of Israel escapted; in the Tribulation they will suffer. The judgement of Egypt was directed against Pharoah, the judgement of the Tribulation Period will be directed against Israel. The Egyptian "Plague of Hail" was what we call today an "ELECTRICAL STORM" and it did not touch the land of Goshen where the children of Israel lived. The fire that ran along the ground was lightning. Now the different between Egyptian Plague and the one John describes is, that in Egypt man and beast suffered with the vegetation, while only the trees and the green grass will suffer when the first Trumpet sounds, and the "HAIL" and "FIRE" will be Mingled with BLOOD, and only one-third of the trees and grass will be burnt up.

SECOND TRUMPET
(The Burning Mountain.) Rev. 8: 8-9

Notice that John does not say that it **was** a "Mountian" that he saw cast into the sea, but that it appeared like a mountain, it was not a burning volcano, but what looked like a meteoric mass on fire. The effect of this "burning mass" on the sea that was probable the Mediterranean Sea; was as close to describing it as John could get. It was to turn a third part of the sea into blood. The "First Egyptian Plague" found in Ex. 7: 19-21 gives the account of the turning of the water of the River Nile into Blood. "And the fish that was in the river died; and the river stank, and the Egyptians could not drank of the water of the river: and there were BLOOD throughout ALL THE LAND OF EGYPT." The difference between the "First Egyptian Plague and the one in the Tribulation Period, is the falling of a "Meteor" into the Mediterranean Sea at the sounding of the second Trumpet; whereby only 1/3 of the sea shall become Blood, that where the "Metor" strikes, and likewise only 1/3 of the living creatures in the sea shall DIE. **1/3 also of the ships** shall be **DESTROYED.**

THIRD TRUMPET

(The Star Wormwood) Rev. 8: 10-11.

When the "Third Trumpet" sounded a **"GREAT STAR"** fell from heaven burning like a lamp. More than likely, this will be another "Meteor," that will assume the form of a "Torch" in its blazing path through the heavens, where they will explode and scatter and will be absorbed by the third part of the rivers and the fountains of waters, and they will be poisoned by the noxious gases, and made bitter, and many men will die from drinking of those waters. It is used in France as a beverage, and is more intoxicating and destructive than ordinary liquors. Jeremiah says in Jer. 9: 13-15 "therefore thus saith the Lord of Hosts, because they have forsaken my law, Behold, I will feed them, even this people (Israel), with **wormwood**, and give them **WATER OF GALL to drink**."

FOURTH TRUMPET.

(SUN, Moon and Stars Smitten.) Rev. 8: 12-13.

What happens under the sounding of this "Trumpet" is similar to what happen under the "Sixth Seal." They are some of the signs spoken of by Christ, in Luke's Godpel, that shall precede His Second Coming. (There shall be signs in the **Sun**, and in the **MOON**, and in the **Stars**, and upon the earth distress of nations, with perplexity; the sea and the waves roaring: And when these things begin to come to pass, then look up, and lift up your heads; for your redemption draweth nigh. Luke 21: 25-28).

Some Versions of the Bible substitute's "**Eagle**" for **ANGEL**, however, that does not effect the meaning.

FIFTH TRUMPET.
FIRST WOE.

(The Plague of Locusts.) Rev. 9: 1-12.

At the sounding of the Fifth Trumpet, John saw a "**STAR**" fall from Heaven. The star was not a literal star, for in the next verse the "**STAR**" is spoken of as a **PERSON (HE)**, AND IN THE Old Testament angels were called "**Stars**." Job 38: 7. Because the "**STAR**" was "**fallen from Heaven**" does not imply that the "ANGEL," (for that is what it was,) a "**Fallen ANGEL**," or **SATAN** himself, as some have believed. John simply meant that he saw the descent of the "**STAR**," or Angel, and so rapidly did it descend that it appeared to be falling. This is the same "**STAR/ANGEL**" that in Rev. 20: 1-3 comes down from Heaven, having the key of the "**BOTTOMLESS PIT**," and a great chain in his hand, and binds **SATAN**, and casts him into the "**PIT**." So this "**STAR/ANGEL**" can not be **SATAN** for he has the key to the "**BOTTOMLESS PIT**," and binds SATAN in it.

THE BOTTOMLESS PIT.

The "**BOTTOMLESS PIT**" is not Hell, or Hades, the place of abode of the "Spirits" of wicked men and women until the resurrection of the "Wicked Dead." Neither is it "Tartarus" the "Prison House" of the "Fallen Angels"(Jude 6-7), nor the "Lake of Fire," the "Final Hell" (Gehenna), Matt. 25: 41, but it is the place of confinement of the **DEMONS**, who are not Satan's Angels but a class of "**disembodied spirits**," believed by many to be the "**disembodied spirits**" of the inhabitants of the Pre-Adamite Earth, who, as they have liberty and opportunity, as in the days of Christ, try to **re-embody** themselves, again in human bodies. They are wicked, unclean, vicious, and have power to derange or to make crazy both mind and body. (Matt. 12:22; 15:22. Luke 4: 35; 8: 26-36; 9: 42.) They are the "Familiar Spirits" of the Old Testament and the "Seducing Spirits" of which Paul warned Timothy. 1Tim. 4: 1 about. They wander about in desolate places. They were used by Christ to illustrate the conditions of the Jewish people in the "last days" when "Demoniacal Power" shall be increased over them SEVENFOLD. Christ said, "When the unclean spirit (or Demon) is come out of a man, the demon walks through dry places, seeking rest, and finds none. Then the unclean Spirit said, I will return into the house from which I came out of: and when he has come, he finds it empty, swept, and cleaned. The unclean spirit then goes and get's to take with him seven other spirits more wicked than himself, and they enter in and dwell there: and the last state of that man is worst than the first. Even so shall it be unto the WICKED GENERATION of the time stated in Matt. 12:43-45 (The Jewish Race). The word generation as presented in Matt. 12: 43-45 is "The average time interval between the birth of parents and the death of their last offspring" which ends the race. So we then see that the Jews, as a "race," at the return of Jesus, will be **"DEMONIACALLY POSSESSED TIMES SEVEN."** This will account for their making a "Covenant with **DEATH and HELL**." Isa. 28: 18. They begged Him to not cast them into the "deep," (that is, not into the "**ABTSS,**" the "**BOTTOMLESS PIT**." Luke 8: 26-36.

The Locusts that John saw coming out of the "Bottomless Pit" were a kind of "**Infernal Cherubim.**" Actually, they were a combination of the **Horse**, the **Man**, the **Woman**, the **Lion**, and the **Scorpion**, and the sound of their wings in flight was as the "sound of chariots of many horses running to battle." Their size is not given in scripture, however they were no doubt much larger than ordinary locusts, but they were not like them. Ordinary locusts ate vegetations, grass and green things; but these locusts were to afflict only men, and they had human intelligence, for they afflicted only those men who had not the "SEAL OF GOD" in their foreheads. They were to torment them for a period of five months.

THE SIXTH TRUMPET SECOND WOE

(The Plague of Horsemen.) Rev. 9: 13-21.

The "Four Angels that was bound at the river Euphrates, was loosed by the SIXTH ANGEL which had the Trumpet, and they were "BAD ANGELS" prepared for a year, and a month, and a day, and an hour, in order to slay the third part of man. They are the leaders of an army of 200,000,000 horsemen. This army is not compose of ordinary men and horses. If you realize that these "Four Angels" were bound at the Euphrates, where Satan's seat was in ancient times, and where it is to be again in the City of Babylon when it is restored; it should be clear that this army is a part of Satan's forces. Supernatural armies are not unknown to the Scriptures. Horses and a **chariot of fire** separated Elijah from Elisha in the day when Elijah was taken up in a whirlwind into Heaven, II Kings 2: 11. When God opened the eyes of Elisha's servant, and he saw the mountians around the city full of horses and chariots of fire. II Kings 6: 13-17. When Jesus Christ shall come to take "The Kingdom," He will be attended by the armies of Heaven, riding on "White Horses," since there is to be war in Heaven, between Jesus Christ and His angels and Satan and his angels (Rev. 12: 7), Satan has among his armies 200,000,000 Horsemen, for no such army of ordinary horsemen ever was, or ever could be assembled on this earth. The "Riders" upon these horses had "Breastplates of **FIRE, JACINTH**, and **BRIMSTONE**," to match the breath of the horses upon which they rode.

The thing about this invasion of "**INFERNAL CAVALRY**" was the awful destruction that came with them. They slew the

THIRD PART OF MEN. If that means the present population at that time, which was app. 1,700,000,000, then this army will destroy 566,666,666 persons. It probably refers to one-third of the men of the old Roman world. One remarkable thing about this destruction is, that the "Four Angels" were prepared and waiting for the EXACT year, month, and day, of 391 days. Thes things and all things are "known only unto God, are all His works from the beginning of the world." Acts 15: 18. This Plague of "**INFERNAL CAVALRY**" was for a twofold purpose, retribution and reformation. To punish the idolatry and demon worship of men, and their sins of murder, sorcery, fornication, and theft, and to keep others from following in their footsteps. But it appears from verses 20 and 21, that the residue of men who were not killed, did not repent and turn from their sins, and so were left for later judgments.

This army of **"INFERNAL CAVALRY,"** will be composed of "**SPIRIT BEINGS**" and they will be invisible to the natural eye, and therefore cannot be resisted, or warred against, by regular weapons used in that day. Those attacked will therefore be without any means of protection, which will account for the awful destruction of human life, for the "third part" of man will be killed. This awful judgement of the "Trumpets" and "Vials" that are to come upon the earth are for the purpose of weeding out the worst of the human race, so that only the better class of persons shall be saved for the millennium.

THE INTERVAL BETWEEN
THE SIXTH AND
SEVENTH TRUMPETS.

----

1. THE LITTLE BOOK. (REV. 10: 1-11.)

Now this **"MIGHTY ANGEL"** refered to in Rev. 10; is believed to be Christ Himself. In the Old Testament the Son of God was called the "ANGEL OF THE LORD" (Ex. 3: 2-18). We are now in that part of the book of Revelation that deals mainly with Israel, and it is what we should expect to hear, Christ spoken of as a "MIGHTY ANGEL." For the description of this "MIGHTY ANGEL" seems to point to the same person that John saw standing in the middle of the "Lampstands" in chapter 1: 12-16, or Christ Himself. That "ANGEL" was clothed in a cloud, there was a RAINBOW upon His head, His face was as it were the SUN, and His feet as PILLARS OF FIRE. There was never an Angel before or since described as this in the scriptures that appeared like that. He is also described as crying with a loud voice, as a lion roareth, and Christ is spoken of in Rev. 5: 5 as "THE LION OF THE TRIBE OF JUDAH"; and in the chapter, the same "MIGHTY ANGEL" speaks of the "Two Witnesses," as "MY WITNESSES," which is further evidence that this "MIGHTY ANGEL" is no other than Christ Himself. For when this "MIGHTY ANGEL" places His right foot upon the sea, and His left foot on the earth, and swears that there shall be "TIME NO LONGER," it is Christ taking formal possession of the Earth and Sea, and declaring that there shall be no longer delay in dispossessing the false claimant of Satan.

When the "MIGHTY ANGEL" cried with a loud voice, this time John heard "SEVEN THUNDERS" utter their voices. These "THUNDERS" spoke, for John heard what they said, and as had been commanded to write what he would see and hear, he proceeded to write what the "voices" of the "SEVEN THUNDERS" uttered, but he was told to "seal up those things which the 'SEVEN THUNDERS' uttered, and write no more." What they said has not as of yet been revealed, but no doubt, will be when the time comes to make the revelation.

John was then told to "Go, take the 'LITTLE BOOK' which is open in the hand of the 'ANGEL' which standeth upon the sea and upon the earth." At this time John was back on the earth, so when John took the "LITTLE BOOK," THE "ANGEL" said to him—"Take, and eat it up; and it shall make thy **belly bitter**, and it shall be in thy mouth **sweet as honey**." And when John had eaten the "BOOK" it was as the "ANGEL" had said,

What was this "LITTLE BOOK"? Was it indeed small? Some claim that it was the "SEVEN SEALED BOOK," now open, and therefore the "TITLE DEED" to the earth, and that the "MIGHTY ANGEL" held it in His hand, as He stood with one foot on the sea and one foot on the earth, as His authority for claiming possession. But the "ANGEL" does not make that use of it, and if it were His "TITLE DEED" to the Earth, it seems very strange that He would give it to John to eat. Also, it is described as a "LITTLE BOOK," as if its contents were small. If that was the case, it stands in marked contrast with the "SEVEN SEALED BOOK" whose numerous "Seals" and the time taken to break them, implies that it was of considerable size. Lets not forget the effect it had upon John of the eating of the "LITTLE BOOK," that seem to indicate that it was more than a "Title Deed." For it contained ingredience that when John first tasted it, the Scripture says "it was sweet as honey to his mouth, but when he had thoroughly digested its contents was bitter to his belly. You see this "LITTLE BOOK" contained information concerning John's work as a Prophet, for the "ANGEL" immediately said to him; "Thou must prophecy again before many people, and nations, and languages, and Kings," which the Scriptures tells us that John did. Now this "LITTLE BOOK," that is now open, is probably the "Book" that Daniel was told to "SEAL UP." Dan. 12: 4, 9. That "LITTLE BOOK" contained information that was not to be revealed until the "TIME OF THE END." Not the "End of Time," but the "End" of the "**TIMES OF THE GENTILES**," which coincides with the last half of Daniel's "**SEVENTIETH WEEK**," and also with "**THE GREAT TRIBULATION PERIOD**." If this supposition be true, then this "LITTLE BOOK" was a foreview of the things that are to come upon Daniel's people in the last half of Daniel's "**SEVENTIETH WEEK**." As John read this "LITTLE BOOK" it seem to confirm this view of the deliverances that were to come to his people, and of the final victory of the Lamb, and the setting up of "The Kingdom," the "Book" was as "**sweet as honey**" to his taste, but when he meditated upon the awful sufferings that would come upon the world, and upon the Jews, under the reign of the "**BEAST**" or Antichrist, and during the pouring out of the "VIALS," it was bitterness to his soul.

We now come to the sounding of the "**MYSTERY OF GOD**" which shall be sounded by the "**SEVENTH TRUMPET ANGEL**" and will finish the work of the "**SEVENTH TRUMPET ANGEL**." Be aware that this is not the "**Mystery of the Church**" for that was finished by the taking out of the Church. That "Mystery" was unknown to the Prophets. The "MYSTERY OF GOD" is the "Mystery" of why God permitted Satan to cause the "Fall of Man" and thus bring sin, and misery, and death into the world. God revealed the fact that in His own time He would make clear "**His MYSTERY**," and when the "**SEVENTH TRUMPET**" sounds, the "**MYSTERY OF GOD" will be finished**, for then the "MYSTERY of INQUITY" will be revealed, (II Thess. 2: 6-10) we know him as the Antichrist, in whom Satan will incarnate himself after he is cast out of Heaven, and in his destruction, and the "Binding of Satan," and the setting up of the "Millennial Kingdom" of Christ, shall fulfill the promises to the Prophets, that peace and righteousness shall reign on the earth. And when, as the result of the "renovation of the earth by fire," the redeemed human race shall take up its abode upon a redeemed and restored earth, and sin and rebellion shall forever be destroyed, the "MYSTERY OF GOD," or why sin was permitted to wreck this world, will be finished.

2. THE TWO WITNESSES. (REV. 11: 1-14).

The "**ANGEL**" that told John to rise and measure the TEMPLE was the same "MIGHTY ANGEL" that handed him the "LITTLE BOOK" TO eat. And as they were both still on the earth, the "TEMPLE" that John was told to measure was the Temple at Jerusalem. Not the Temple of Herod, for that had been destroyed over 25 years before by Titus, in A. D. 70. This then must be a future temple that is to be built at Jerusalem during the reign of Antichrist, for he shall sit in it, and proclaim himself GOD. II Thess. 2: 3,4. And he shall cause the "ABOMINATION OF DESOLATION" spoken of by Daniel the Prophet (Dan. 9: 27), propably the "IMAGE OF THE BEAST," to be set up in the "HOLY PLACE." Matt. 24: 15. This will not be the Millennial Temple described by Ezekiel (Ez. 4: 1; 42: 20), for that will be built at Shiloh, in the midst of the Holy Oblation (Ez. 48: 8, 21), and not until after the physical changes that will take place at the return of Christ (Zech. 14: 4); shall have changed the surface of the land of Palestine. The Temple that the Jews will build on their return to Jerusalem will probably be destroyed by the Earthquake that destroyed by the Earthquake that destroys the tenth part of the City, for that Earthquake will coincide with the "Great Earthquake" that shall occur at the breaking of the "Seventh Seal," the sounding of the "Seventh Trumpet," and the pouring out of the "Seventh Vial." (Rev. 8: 5, 11: 19, 16: 18).

John was told to measure only the Temple proper,(That part of the temple that was standard or required.) and to leave out the "Court" that surrounded it. The Temple of Herod had four Courts: the Court of the Priests, the Court of Israel, the Court of the Women and the Court of the Gentiles. The Tabernacle had but one Court; while Solomon's Temple had two, the Court of the Priests, and the Court of the Gentiles. Since the court of this new Temple, a nd the Holy City Jerusalem, is to be trodden under foot of the Gentiles for 42 months, or 3 ½ years, this period must refer to the **last half** of the "Seventieth Week," after Antichrist breaks his "Covenant" with the Jews, and desecrates the Temple, for Jerusalem must be trodden down of the Gentiles until the "Times of the Gentiles" is fulfilled (Luke 21: 24), and that will not end until the Battle of Armageddon.

After the "MIGHTY ANGEL" had given John instructions as to measuring the Temple, He said; "And I will give power unto MY "TWO WITNESSES," and they shall prophesy a "thousand, two hundred and threescore days" equaling 42 months of 3o days each, or 3 ½ years, then the time when these "**Two Witnesses**" are to prophesy must coincide with the last half of the **"Week,"** or the time of **THE GREAT TRIBULATION**.

Now let's take a look at these "TWO WITNESSES," Who are they? They are men: No not system, or Churches, or a body of witnesses, for they prophesy and are clothed in sackcloth, neither of which can be said of other than persons, and these are TWO of them. It is very easy to identify them. They have power to shut heaven that it rain not in the **DAYS OF THEIR PROPHECY.** This can only be referring to Elijah, who had power in the days of King Ahab to shut up the heavens for the space of three years and six months (I Kings 17: 1; Luke 4: 25; James 5: 17), and this is the same length of time, 42 months, or 1260 days, or 3 ½ years, that these "TWO WITNESSES" are to prophesy. We also know that Elijah was translated, and did not see death, that he might come back before "THE GREAT AND DREADFUL DAY OF THE LORD" for the purpose of "turning the heart of the children to their fathers," and this is the purpose of the prophesying of these "TWO

WITNESSES." Mal. 4: 5-6. When the Prophet Malachi said that Elijah would come again, just before "the Great And Dreadful Day Of The Lord," we know that this prophecy was not fulfilled in John The Baptist. The first coming of Christ was announced, but no :Great And Dreadful Day Of The Lord" followed. That event is yet future, and follows the testimony of these "TWO WITNESSES."

The Jews sent Priests and Levities from Jerusalem to ask John The Baptist if he was the Christ? He confessed--- "I AM NOT THE CHRIST." And they followed with, "What Then? Art thou Elijah?" And he said ---"I AM NOT." So we must except the fact that John's answer to these questions means that he was NOT ELIJAH. When Gabriel announced to Zacharias the birth of John the Baptist, he said, he shall go before Christ in the "**SPIRIT AND POWER**" OF Elijah. Meaning that he will not be Elijah, but shall be like him in **spirit** and **power**. John who was in prison, sent messengers to Jesus to ask Him if He were the Christ, after Christ had dismissed those messengers He said to the multitude of John, "IF YE WILL RECEIVE 'IT,' THIS IS ELIJAH WHICH WAS FOR TO COME." Matt. 11: 1-14. What did Jesus mean by "IT"? The contexts shows that that Jesus was talking about the "KINGDOM" (VERSE 11, 12), AND IF THEY HAD RECEIVED "the kingdom" that John announced was at hand, then John, instead of being John, would have been ELIJAH come back, but because God foresaw that the Jews would not receive the KINGDOM, He would not send ELIJAH at that time, so He had to send a substitute with the "spirit" and "power" of Elijah in his place, so He sent John the Baptist. Jesus had said to the disciples when they were coming down from the Mt. of Ttansfiguration, where they had seen Elijah, that Elilah shall come first and restore all things. And now Jesus is telling them that "ELIAS IS COME ALREADY," and they knew him not, but have done unto him whatsoever they wanted. Then the Disciples understood that He spake unto them about 'JOHN THE BAPTIST'. Matt. 17: 11-13.

Now whatever this may mean, it cannot contradict John's own declaration that he **WAS NOT ELIJAH**, or Christ's statement that if God had **foreseen** that the Jews would have received the Kingdom, He would have sent **ELIJAH** instead of John. And Christ's statement in the above reference, that Elijah's purpose in coming is to "RESTORE ALL THINGS," which John did not do, and Malachi's declaration that Elijah would not come until just before the 'GREAT AND DREADFUL DAY OF THE LORD,' makes it clear that John the Baptist was not Elijah, and that Elijah is yet to come.

It appears that one of the "TWO WITNESSES" will be Elijah, but who the other one will be is not yet known. Many claim that Moses will be the second Witness, while some say he will be Enoch, because they say that Moses, being a resurrected person cannot die again, and the "Two Witnesses" are both to die. It's believed that both Enoch and Eliijah were caught up in their bodies, without dying, that they mightcome back again in their bodies and die. However, there is no scriptural reference for declaring that Moses cannot die again. Lazarus was raised from the dead and he died again, and the "Wicked Dead" shall be raised from the dead, and after the "Great White Throne judgement," they shall be sentenced to die again, which is the "SECOND DEATH." Rev. 20: 12-15.

It is said of these "**TWO WITNESSES**" that they have power---

1. "To **SHUT HEAVEN**, that it **RAIN NOT** in the days of their prophecy."
2. "And have power over **WATERS** to **TURN THEM TO BLOOD**, and to smite the earth with **ALL PLAGUES**, as often as they will."

Now we know that moses had power to turn water into **BLOOD**, and to smite the earth with **PLAGUES**, but we are not told that Enoch had such power.

When we study what shall happen durning the period of the "**TWO WITNESSES**" which will be the last half of the "week," or 3 ½ years, we will see that the "**TWO WITNESSES**" can be none other than **MOSES** and **ELIJAH**. No doubt **ELIJAH** will shut up the heavens that there shall be no rain, during the period (3 ½ years) of their witnessing, because there is to be a "**FIRE TEST**" like the one Elijah appointed on Mt. Carmel in the days of King Ahab (I. Kings 18: 17-40), and the contest will be between **Elijah** and the "**FALSE PROPHET**," and the "**FALSE PROPHET**" shall have power to do what the Priests of Baal could not do, bring **FIRE FROM HEAVEN**. (Rev. 13: 13). The question on Mt. Carmel was, "Who is God, **JEHOVAH** or **BAAL**?" In the days of Antichrist it will be, "Who is God, JEHOVAH or ANTICHRIST?" The test will be the power to bring down FIRE FROM HEAVEN. This "False Prophet" will imitate the power of Elijah and bring down FIRE FROM HEAVEN, however, the test will not be decisive. The true followers of God's Israelites will continue to acknowledge the claim of Jehovah, while the followers of "The Beast" will continue to believe in him. But Elijah shall not be as fortunate as he was in the days of Ahab, because then he escaped the vengeance of Jezebel, but he will not be able to escape the vengeance of Antichrist who will see to it that both he and Moses are slain.

There are four Plagues that are to accompany the pouring out of the "Vials," that are similar to the "Plagues of Egypt," Since the evidence seems conclusive that the "TWO WITNESSES" were **Moses** and **Elijah**; and Elijah did not escape the vengeance of Antichrist; then **Moses** is most likely to bring the "Plagues" to pass.

The "**TITLE**" of these two men were given to them by the "**MIGHTY ANGEL**" Christ Himself, He call them My "**TWO WITNESSES**." This implies that they were in the business of "**WITNESSING**." When we look forward to their witnessing on the Mt. of Transfiguration (Matt. 17: 3), and that it was TWO MEN that witnessed to the women at the

Tomb that Jesus had risen (Luke 24: 4-7), and that it was TWO MEN who stood by and witnessed to the Disciples as Jesus ascended into Heaven (Acts 1: 10-11), and that in all three incidents the men were clothed in "**Shining garments,**" it seems clear that Moses was resurrected and Elijah translated for the express business of "**WITNESSING FOR CHRIST.**"

These "**TWO WITNESSES**" are called the "**TWO OLIVE TREES**" and the "**TWO CANDLESTICKS**" which stand before the God of the earth. By turning back to the Old Testament, we will find that the Prophet Zechariah saw in a dream a "**GOLDEN CANDLESTICK,**" with a bowl upon the top of it, and the seven lamps thereon, and seven pipes to the seven lamps; and TWO OLIVE TREES by it, one upon the right side of the bowl, and the other upon the left side thereof. And he turned to the angel that talked with him and said "What are these "TWO OLIVE TREES' upon the right side of the CANDLESTICK and upon the left side thereof?" and he said, "These are the "TWO ANOINTED ONES,' that stand by the Lord of the whole earth." Zech. 4: 1- 14. These "TWO ANOINTED ONES" were Zerubbabel the Governor, and Joshus the High Priest. Haggai 1: 1, 14. Zech. 3: 1; 4: 6. They had been anointed by the Holy Spirit to rebuild and restore Jerusalem and the Temple after the Babylonian Captivity, against which Satan was raising up much opposition. Zech. 3: 1-7. Zerubbabel and Joshua are types of the "TWO WITNESSES" whose work it will be to proclaim that the time has come to rebuild Jerusalem and re-establish the Temple worship, for the "KINGDOM OF HEAVEN" is at hand. And they will have to do in the face of the opposition of Satan, who at that time will have incarnated himself in the Antichrist. This illustrates the fact that every type in the Scriptures has its Anti-Type, and that the Old Testament infolds and unfolds the New Testament, and that the Anti-Type appears the plan and purpose of God remains unfulfilled and incomplete.

These "TWO WITNESSES" are to prophecy for 3 ½ years, and for that length of time they are immune from death. For if any man attempt to hurt them, "fire will proceed out of their mouths and destroy their enemies." But when they have finished their testimony, they shall be overcome by "THE BEAST" (Antichrist), who shall kill them, and their dead bodies shall lie in the streets of Jerusalem, for "**three and a half days**" (Ezek. 23: 3-4, 8, 19), and the people shall not suffer their dead bodies to be buried, and they shall rejoice over them, because these "**TWO WITNESSES**" who tormented them by their testimony and their plagues are dead.

However, the people's rejoicing will be short-lived, for at the end of the 3 ½ days, the "SPIRIT OF LIFE" will re-enter the bodies of the "TWO WITNESSES," and they shall stand upon their feet, and great fear shall be upon their enemies, and a voice from Heaven will be heard saying---"COME UP HITHER," and they shall ascend up to Heaven in a cloud as Christ Himself ascended, and their enemies shall witness their ascent. They are first resurrected and then translated. And the same hour of their ascension there will be a "Great Earthquake" that will destroy a **tenth part of the city of Jerusalem** and 7000 of its inhabitants, and the remainder of its inhabitants will turn to God from fright. But this repentance will be short—lived, like that of Pharoah's.

The "TWO WITNESSES" description is given to John in the "INTERVAL" between the "Sixth" and "Seventh" Trumpets, and they testified for 1260 days or 42 months, so there witnessing was still future when John was told about them, for the "MIGHTY ANGEL" said to John, "I WILL give," which let's us know that the "TWO WITNESSES" had not as yet appeared, for John did not see them, he only recorded what the "MIGHTY ANGEL" told him about them. We have seen that the period of their witnessing is during the "last half" of the Week, which means that they do not appear until the "Middle" of the Week.

3. SEVENTH TRUMPET. THIRD WOE

(Covers The Rest Of The Week.) Rev. 11: 15-19.

The sounding of the "SEVENTH TRUMPET" includes all that happens down to chapter 20: 3. When it sounded, John heard "Great Voices" in Heaven saying---"THE KINGDOMS OF THIS WORLD ARE BECOME THE KINGDOMS OF OUR LORD, AND OF HIS CHRIST; AND HE SHALL REIGN FOR EVER AND EVER." This is the announcement that the time had come for Christ to take "THE KINGDOM," though "The Kingdom" does not fully come into His possession for 3 ½ years. The whole of this passage is **anticipative,** for the "sayings" of the Four and Twenty Elders look forward to the resurrections and Judgements of Rev. chapter 20. The scene is located in Heaven. For it is there that John hears the Trumpet sound, and sees the "Temple of God" opened, and hears the voices and thunderings that accompany the devastation of the earth by "earthquake" and "hail." This preliminary announcement is followed by the great events, which will be the most momentous and no doubt remarkable events that has ever happen on this earth.

The "**THIRD WOE**" includes the "**VIALS**," and all other judgements down to Rev. chapter 20: 3. We find in Rev. Chapter 10: 7, that "The time limit of the "**SEVENTH TRUMPET**" is spoken of as "**THE DAYS**'" of the "voice" of the "**SEVENTH ANGEL**" when he shall begin to sound. Implying that the blast or blasts, of the "**SEVENTH TRUMPET**" is to be extended over the whole of the last half of the "Week."

THE MIDDLE OF THE WEEK

THE SEVEN PERSONAGES

1. THE SUN-CLOTHED WOMAN.

Rev. 12: 1-2.

In the "Middle of the Week" two "**Wonders**" (or SIGNS) will appear in Heaven, for John is now back in Heaven, however, they are actually "**SYMBOLS**" of something, and should be therefore interpreted. The first will be a "**SUN CLOTHED WOMAN.**" Who does this "Sun Clothed Woman" represent? There are those who believe that this Woman represents the Virgin Mary, Others believes that she represents the Church. Those who say she represents the Church claim that she represents the visible or outward Church, and her "child" represents the "True Church" or those who are to be "caught out" at the Rapture. Well the fact is, the "SUN CLOTHED Woman is neither the Virgin Mary or the Church. She is ISRAEL. When we take a look AT Gen. 37, we are reminded of "**Joseph's dream,**" where he says "Behold, I have dreamed a dream more; and behold, the 'SUN' and the 'MOON' and the 'ELEVEN STARS' made Obeisance to me," we can see the Jewish character of this woman, for Joseph was to be the "Twelfth" star.

Israel is often compared to a woman, and a married woman, in the Old Testament Isa. 54: 1. And in the period of her rejection she is spoken of as a WIDOW (Isa. 47: 7-9. Luke 18: 1-8), and a DIVORCED Woman (Isa. 50: 1), and an ADULTEROUS WIFE (Jer. 3: 1-25, Hosea 2: 1-23) but the Church is a VIRGIN, and an ESPOUSED Virgin at that. IICor. 11: 2. Eph. 5: 25-27. The "Sun Clothed Woman" is described as being "WITH CHILD," and "TRAVAILING

83

TO BRING FORTH." Now when was the Church in such a condition? To be found in such a condition would unfit her to be the Bride of Christ. And check this out; nowhere in the scriptures is it stated that the Church is ever to be a **Mother**. But it is so prophesied of Israel. The Apostle Paul asked the question, speaking of the sevenfold privilege of Israel, "who are Israelites; to whom pertaineth the adoption, and the glory, and the covenants, and the giving of the law, and the service of God, and the promises, whose are the fathers, and of whom **AS CONCERNING THE FLESH CHRIST CAME**." Rom. 9: 4-5. We see here that Christ was to come from **ISRAEL**. Then we know that the "PROMISED SEED" was to come through ISRAEL, and the prophet Isaiah looked forward to the time when Israel could say "**UNTO US A CHILD IS BORN UNTO US A SON IS GIVEN**." Isa. 9: 6-7. Before the promised heir could be born Israel had to pass through many afflictions and judgements. These were her "TRAVAIL DAYS." Therefore, there can be no question but that the "Sun Clothed Woman" represents **ISRAEL.**

2. THE DRAGON.
Rev. 12: 3-4.

The second **"WONDER"** that will appear in Heaven will be a "**GREAT RED DRAGON.**" We are not left in doubt as to who is meant, for in verse 9 he is called that old "**OLD SERPENT, THE DEVIL**," and "**SATAN.**" His color ie RED, the color of blood, for he was a murderer from the beginning. John 8: 44.

He has "SEVEN HEADS" and "TEN HORNS," and upon his heads are "SEVEN CROWNS." These are the emblems of the universality of his earthly dominion, and typify the sevenfold perfection of his power: for he is the PRINCE OF THE "POWERS OF THE AIR." And the "PRINCE OF THIS WORLD."

(Eph. 6: 12; John 12: 31, 14: 30, 16: 11.)

As such Jesus did not dispute his claim when in the wilderness temptation, he offered Him the "Kingdoms of this world" and the glory of them. Luke 4: 5-7. His "seven heads," "Ten Horns," and "Crowns," associates him with the "**BEAST OUT OF THE SEA**" of the first verse of the next chapter, the only difference being that the Dragon's "Crowns" are on his "Heads," while those of the beast are on his "Horns," and therefore differ in numbers. These features are common to both and reveals the fact that there is some relation between the "Dragon" and the "Beast," and that the "Beast" is an earthly embodiment or incarnation of the "DRAGON," FOR THE Beast does not appear on earth until after the "Dragon" is cast out of Heaven. Now the "Antichrist" exists from the beginning of the week, but he does not become the "BEAST" until in the "middle of the week." Satan is now cast out of Heaven and incarnates himself into the "BEAST." Then the "Antichrist" breaks his "Covenant" with Israel, and desecrates the Temple, and becomes the "Satanic Person" that rules during the last half of the week.

The Antichrist will have the "**STARS OF HEAVEN**" attached to his **"tail,"** which reveals the fact that Satan will take with him in his expulsion from Heaven, a third of the angels, for the angels are spoken of as "Stars" in the Old Testament. (Job 38: 7). These "Angels" will be cast out with him into the earth, and at some point in time, They will secretly sow the seeds of rebellion, and ultimately they will be cast with Satan into the "Lake of Fire" which will be prepared for them. (Matt. 25:41). These Angels must be bound with Satan in the "bottomless Pit," for during the Millennium they do not appear to be present on the earth.

John tells us that the "Dragon" stood before the "Sun Clothed Woman" ready to "devour her child" as soon as it was born. It is interesting to trace in the scriptures the story of Satan's efforts to prevent the **birth** of the "Man-Child" **CHRIST**, and then after his birth to destroy Him before He could reach the cross and purchase man's redemption. As soon as Satan had accomplished the fall of Adam and Eve, he found himself under the curse of God, and was told that the "**Seed**" of the Woman would bruise his head. (Gen. 3: 14-15). This aroused the enmity in Satan and he determined to prevent the birth of the promised "Seed," or, if that were not possible, to destroy the "Seed" after His birth. So as soon as Abel was born, from whom the promised "Seed" was to come, Satan schemed for his destruction, and finally got his brother Cain to kill him. Then the "Sons of God" (who were Angels) no doubt at Satan's instigation, married the "Daughters of Men" (Cainites), and their "sin," and the character of their offspring moved God to destroy mankind from off the earth; that was what Satan planned for, and it would have been a victory for Satan, so God decided to spare the race, and begin over again with a representative man, Noah. But when Noah's journey ended on Mt. Ararat, it was not long before Noah planted a vineyard and drank himself drunk with the wine from the vineyard. The result was the curse of Canaan the Son of Ham. (Gen. 9: 18-27). Then the people began to multiply and Satan filled their heart with pride and presumption and they rose and built the "Tower of Babel," the result this time was the "Confusion of Tongues" and the unity of the race broken up. (Gen. 11: 1-9). Then the Lord called Abraham and the fight narrowed down to his seed. Abraham was 75 years old and had no children, and Sarah his wife was 65 years of age and barren. (Gen. 16: 1). Now Satan laughed at this situation due to Sarah's barrenness, in which probably he had a hand in, but God decieded to show Satan that He could work a miracle whenever necessary, to produce the promised "seed," so God waited until Sarah was 90 years old (Gen. 17: 17), and then He caused her to conceive and bear the promised "seed." (Gen. 18: 9-15; 21: 1-3). When Isaac was about 12 years old, Satan moved God to test Abraham by commanding him to offer up Isaac as a sacrifice upon Mount Moriah. It was similar to the test of Job, given in Job 1: 6-12; 2: 3-6. The plan for Isaac's destruction failed, for when God saw that Abraham was ready and willing to slay his son, He intervened and spared his life. When Isaac grew up and married Rebekah, Satan, in order to prevent her from having Children, caused her to be barren, but Isaac prayed and God heard his prayer (Gen. 25: 20-21), and twins were born. Then Satan, when they had grown up, stirred up enmity between them, hoping that the tragedy of Cain and Abel would be repeated, and Jacob, the seed through whom Christ was to come, would be slain. Now you would think that Satan would give up, trying to keep God from carrying out His will, but when the time came for Moses to be born, Satan put it into the heart of Pharaoh to order that all male Hebrew Children should be put to death at birth, his purpose was to destroy the male line of descent altogether. However, Satan's plan was interrupted by a baby's tear. (Ex. 2: 5-10). So the plan continued on until at the death of King Jehoshaphat, when his son Jehoram slew all his brethren with the sword (II Chron. 21: 13), thus reducing the "Royal Seed" down to one life. But Jehoram had children also. Then the Arabians slew all his children but one, Ahaziah the youngest. (II Chron. 21: 17). And Ahaziah had children also. And the killings went on and on, and these in turn were slain by Athaliah his mother, who at the instigation of Satan thought she had slain them all, but God decided to rescue the infant son at the hands of his aunt, who hid him in the Temple (II Cor. 22: 10-12), and for 6 years all the hope's of God's people as to the promised "seed" rested on that infant's life. During the Captivity, Satan tried to destroy the whole Hebrew nation at the hands of Haman, but a very small thing as a king's sleepless night, interfeared with that plan. (Esther 3: 8-15, 6: 1-11).

At last the promised "**SEED**" was born. Then Satan, failing to prevent His birth, determined to destroy Him before He could reach the cross. To that end he prompted Herod, through jealousy and fear, to slay all the male children at Bethlehem under 2 years old, but Joseph warned of God in a dream, had fled with the infant Christ to Egypt. When Christ enter into His ministry Satan met Him in the wilderness and suggested that He throw Himself from the Pinnacle of the Temple. Foiled in that Satan sought Christ's life by getting His own townspeople to attempt to cast Him over a precipice. (Luke 4: 29). The two storms on the sea of Galilee were but attempts of Satan to destroy Christ. Take at look at this; "You can not rebuke a thing, you can only reburke a person," and when Christ rebuked the winds and the sea, He rebuked the **person** (Satan) who had caused their disturbance. (Matt. 8: 24-27).

Satan now renews the fight through Pharisees and Priests until he finally succeeds in getting one of Christ's own disciples Judas, to sell out his Master. He then sought to Kill Christ. And when he had finally succeeded in having Christ crucified, with the aide of Pilate, Satan wanted to make sure of no suprises, so he though to made sure by having the place of burial sealed and guarded. But when Christ rose from the dead, Satan's rage knew no bounds. Of course, Satan and his angels contested the Ascension of Christ, for only then can we account for the necessity of going up 10 days before Pentecost, that He might have ample time, (convoyed by Twelve Legions of Angels,) for any "**Battle of the Clouds**" that Satan might attempt. The history of the Christian Church, even including now, is but one long story of the "Irrepressible Conflict" between Satan and God's people.

In I Thess. 2: 18 Paul says "We would have come unto you, even I Paul, once and again, but SATAN hindered us." And now as the time draws nigh for Christ to receive "The Kingdom," which means thatHe will come back to the earth, and that Satan's power and dominion over the earth shall cease, and Satan will be bound for 1000 years, and Satan filled with wrath will oppose His return with his armies and there will be "**WAR IN HEAVEN**."

3. THE MAN CHILD.

Rev. 12: 5-6.

As the result of her "**Travail**" the "**Sun Clothed Woman**" brought forth a "**MAN-CHILD**" who was to rule the nations with a "**ROD OF IRON**." There can be no question as to who is meant by the "Man-Child." He is **CHRIST**. The Second Psalm settles that—"Ask of me, and I shall give thee the for thine inheritance, and the uttermost parts of the earth for thy possession. Thou shalt break them with a '**ROD OF IRON**': Thou shalt dash them in pieces like a potter's vessel." The "Man-Child" cannot be the Church, as some claim, because the "Man-Child" is caught up to the FATHER'S THRONE, where He is now seated, while the Church, which is not as yet caught up, but is to be caught up to CHRIST IN THE AIR. (I. Thess. 4: 17).

Those who claim that Christ and the Church together constitutes the "Man-Child," because in the message to the Church at Thyatira, the promise is to the "Overcomers," that they shall rule the nations with a "**ROD OF IRON**," This promise is not to the Church as a whole, but only to the "Overcomers" of the "Thyatiran Church Period," A. D. 606-1520. In other words the "Overcomers" of the "Thyatiran Church Period" shall hold some prominent "**Ruling Power**" with Christ in the Millennial Kingdom.

"And the 'WOMAN' fled into the 'wilderness,' where she hath a place prepared of God, that they should feed her there a thousand two hundred and threescore days."

(Read Carefully)---Here is where many interpreters of this Chapter have been led astray. They seem to think that the "Woman" flees into the wilderness immediately after the birth of her child, and because the time of her flight is in the "Middle of the Week" (note: The 1260 days of her preservation in the wilderness corresponds with the "last half" of the "Week"), They cannot see how her "**Child**" can be Christ, because Christ was born and "caught up" to His Father's Throne centuries ago, while this event is still future. They somehow over looked the fact that between the 5th and 6th verses of this chapter the present CHURCH PERIOD comes in. Between these verses the "GAP" between the "Sixty-ninth" and the "Seventieth" Week of Daniel's "Seventy Weeks" is found. Now the fifty describes the "BIRTH" of Christ, and His **"ASCENSION,"** and then John jumps over the "GAP," and describes in the 6th verse the "Flight" of the Woman **ISRAEL** into the wilderness to escape from the Antichrist. The reason for this is that John is not dealing here with the Church, and having introduced the "Woman" and her "Child" to account for the "Dragon's" wrath against her because he did not succeed in destroying her "Child" (Christ) when He was born, John jumps over the "GAP," that he may again take up God's dealing with ISRAEL. The "Flight" of the "Woman" is mentioned here by anticipation, for she does not flee until after the "War in Heaven."

Here is evidence that the "Sun Clothed Woman" is not the "Virgin Mary," for she does not flee into Egypt, as Joseph and the Virgin did (Matt. 2: 12-15), but into the WILDERNESS. Neither does she flee "with her child," for it was taken away from her and caught up to the "Throne of God." Neither does she flee for her child's protection, but for her **own safety.**

We are told in this passage that Christ's Millennial rule will be **AUTOCRATIC**, for He shall rule over the Nations with a "**ROD OF IRON**." This does not signify that His rule will be tyrannical. It simply means that His **WILL** shall be supreme. We cannot imagine Christ's rule to be other than a rule of love. Politics will have no place in the government, the masses will not be oppressed by those in power, equal rights will be accorded to everyone, and every man shall sit under his **own vine and figtree.**

4. THE ARCHANGEL.

(War In Heaven.) Rev. 12: 7-12.

The "**WAR IN HEAVEN**" is started by the attempt to expel the DRAGON and his angels **From the Heavenlies**. That the **DRAGON** (Satan) and his angels were not cast out of Heaven at the time of his "Rebellion" (which antedates the present earth), and was confined in some "prison house," is clear, for he was at liberty to visit the garden of Eden and tempt Adam and Eve, and he had access to God in Heaven in the days of Job, 2000 years before Christ (Job 1:1; 2: 8), and he was free to visit the earth in Christ's day and tempt Him in the wilderness, and later to sift Peter. His origin is more or less sheltered in mystery, but one thing is for sure, he is a "**created being**," and that of the most exalted type. He was before his rebellion the guardian or protector of the "Throne of God," The "**Anointed Cherub that Covereth.**" He was perfect in all his ways from the day that he was created until iniquity was found in him. In him was the fullness of wisdom, and the perfection of beauty, but it was his "**beauty**" that caused the **pride** (I Tim. 3: 6) that was his downfall. He dwelt in Eden, the Garden of God. This does not refers to the earthly Eden, but to the "Paradise of God" on high, for Satan dwelt on the "Holy Mount of God." This can be founded in Ezek. 28: 11-19, where the prophet has a "foreview" of the Antichrist under the title of the "King of Tyrus," and as Antichrist when he becomes the "Beast" shall be an **incarnation of Satan,** the Prophet here describes Satan's original glory from which he fell, for there has never as yet been such a King of Tyrus as here described.

It is noted here that the one here called "**LUCIFER**," is also called the "**King of Babylon,**" (Isa. 14: 4). As there never has been a King of Babylon like the one here described, the description must be that of a future King of Babylon. Since Antichrist is to have for his Capital City the rebuilded Babylon, this is probably a "foreview" by the prophet of Antichrist when he was indwelt by "**LUCIFER**" in that day when he shall be King of Babylon, and also King of Tyrus.

The common notion is that Satan and his angels are imprisoned in Hell. However, this is not true. The angels described in II Pet. 2: 4, and Jude 6, as having left their "**first astate**," and being "**reserved in everlasting chains under darkness**," are not Satan's angels. They are a special class of angels, spoken of as "Sons of God," whose sin of marrying the "Daughters of Men" caused the flood. (Gen. 6: 1-8.) They are the "Spirits in Prison" of whom Peter speaks of in I. Peter 3: 18-20. They are now confined in "Tartarus" awaiting the "Great White Throne" Judgement. Jude 6. As this book of Revelation that we are now studying is a prophecy of "**Things to come**" that was future in the Apostle John's day, and it declares that Satan was still in the Heavenlies at that time, A. D. 96, since he has not been cast out, he must still be there. Satan is the Ruler of the "Power of Darkness" of the "Spirit world" (Eph. 6: 11-12), and his position is so exalted that even Michael the Archangel dare not insult him. Jude 9. So mighty is he that man cannot successfully resist him without Divine help.

Satan is a **King,** and has a **KINGDOM**. Of it Christ said—"If Satan cast out Satan he is divided against himself; how then shall his '**KINGDOM**' stand"? (Matt. 12: 24-30.) Speaking of the "Evil Powers" Paul wrote—"We wrestle not against flest and blood, but against 'Principalities,' against '**Spiritual Wickedness**' in **HIGH PLACES"** (the Heavenlies). (Eph. 6: 12). From this we see that Satan's Kingdom consists of "**Principalities**," "**Powers**," "**Age Rulers of Darkness**," and "**Wicked Spirits**" in the Heavenlies. These "Principalities" are ruled by "Princes" who control the nations of the earth in the days of Daniel the Prophet, when a heavenly Messenger was sent to Daniel, but was hindered "three weeks" from reaching him by the "**Prince of the Kingdom of Persia**," Satan's ruling "prince of Persia," until Michael the Archangel came to rescue him. Dan. 10: 10-14.

The "Commanders in Chief" of the "War in Heaven" will be **MICHAEL** (the Archangel) and the **DRAGON** (Satan). Michael shows up first in the book of Daniel, and his appearance here is confirmation that this part of the Book of Revelation is Jewish, and a continuation or supplement to the book of Daniel. Michael is called in the book of Daniel "**one of the CHIEF PRINCES**" (Dan. 10: 13), "**YOUR PRINCE**" (Dan. 10: 21), and the "**GREAT PRINCE WHICH STANDETH FOR THY PEOPLE.**" (Dan. 12: 1). When means that Michael had been chosen from among the "Chief Princes" that stand before God, to be the protector of Daniel's people, the Jews. In Jude 9 he is called the "**ARCHANGEL**," Since there is but one "Archangel" spoken of in the Bible, Michel must be that one. He also has something to do with the resurrection of the dead, for he is associated with the "resurrection" mentioned in Dan. 12: 1-2, and he contested with the Devil the resurrection of Moses (Jude 9), and the "**Voice**" of the Archangel that will be heard when the "Dead in Christ" shall rise(I Thess. 4: 16), will be the "voice" of MICHAEL.

When the "Dragon" is cast out of the "Heavenlies" there will be great rejoicing in Heaven because the "**Accuser**" of Christ's "**Brethren**" (the Jews) is cast down, but there will be "**woe**" for the "**inhabitants of the earth**," for the "Dragon" will be filled with "great wrath" because he knows that he will have but a "**short time**" (3 ½ years) to vent his wrath on the inhabitants of the earth before he is chained and cast into the Bottomless Pit.

While Satan has been the "Accuser of the brethren" in all ages, reference is here made to the "**Jewish Remnant**" (the brethren of Christ), who during the first 3 ½ years of the "Tribulation Period," a period of unparalleled suffering which, according to premillennial eschatology, will precede the establishment of the future Kingdom of Israel (Acts 1; 6). Jermiah the Prophet specifically calls this time "the time of Jacob's trouble" (Jer. 30: 7). It will involve the Jewish people who will have gone back to Palestine in unbelief, and they died as "martyrs." As they overcame by the "**Blood Of The Lamb**," then the "**TIME**" of their overcoming must be subsequent to the shedding of Christ's blood on Calvary, therefore, Satan according to this account, could not have been cast out of the "Heavenlies" prior to the Crucifixion of Christ. When Jesus said— "I beheld Satan as lightning **fall from heaven**" (Luke 10: 18), He was not referring to some past fall of Satan, but it was a prophetic utterance, by way of anticipation, of his future fall, when Satan shall be hurled headfirst out of Heaven by Michael the Archangel. Daniel the Prophet also tells us that Satan's casting out will be at the "**Time of Trouble**" that is to come upon Daniel's People, the Jews, and that "**Time of Trouble**" is the "**GREAT TRIBULATION.**" At that time Michael shall "stand up" to deliver Daniel's People, and the result will be "WAR IN HEAVEN" and Daniel's People shall be delivered, not from the "Great Tribulation," but out of it. When the Dragon and all the Principalities and powers of evil that at that time occupied the "Middle Heaven" of the Heavenlies; that is the Heaven between the atmosphere of our earth, and the "Third Heaven" where God dwells, are cast out and down, then the Heavens will be CLEAN, for they were not then clean in God's sight. (Job 15: 15). All of these "Evil Powers" will no doubt be imprisoned during the millennium, with Satan, the Heavens will be CLEAN during that period, and this will account for the universal rule of righteousness and peace of those days.

"THE PERSECUTION OF THE SUN CLOTHED WOMAN"

Rev. 12: 13-16.

After reading the above Scriptures, you should note the symbolism in the names ascribed to the characters.

When the Dragon is cast out of Heaven into the earth, knowing that his defeat has been brought about by the elevation of the "**MAN-CHILD**" to the place of power, he will concentrate his hatred and malice on the "Sun-Clothed Woman" (who is Israel), who gave the "Man-Child" birth. To the "Woman" will be given the "**WINGS OF A GREAT EAGLE**" that she may fly into the "Wilderness," into "**HER**

PLACE" where she shall be nourished for **3 ½ years.** Now this takes us back to the flight of Israel from Egypt, of which God said---"Ye have seen what I did unto the Egyptians, and how I bare you on 'EAGLE'S WINGS,' and brought you unto myself." (EX. 19: 4). As the "Woman" and the "Dragon" are symbols, so are the "Eagle's Wings." They speak of the rapid and safe flight of the "Woman" or ISRAEL into the "Wilderness" where she shall be safely kept and nourished for 3 ½ years until the Dragon is bound.

Isaiah speaks of this time in Isa. 26: 20-21; 27: 1, when he says---"Come, my people (ISRAEL) enter thou into thy CHAMBERS, and SHUT THY DOORS ABOUT THEE: HIDE THYSELF AS IT WERE FOR A LITTLE WHILE (3 ½ years) UNTIL THE INDIGNATION (The Great Tribulation) BE OVERPAST. FOR, BEHOLD, THE LORD COMETH OUT OF HIS PLACE TO PUNISH THE INHABITANTS OF THE EARTH FOR THEIR INIQUITY. . . . In THAT DAY the Lord with His sore and great and strong sword shall punish 'LEVIATHAN' the piercing SERPENT, even 'LEVIATHAN' THE crooked SERPENT, and He shall slay 'THE DRAGON' that comes up out of the sea." (Rev. 13: 1-2).(read also Matt. 24: 15-22; Dan. 9: 27).

A careful comparison of the previous two passages will reveal their difference. Luke refers to the "Destruction of Jerusalem" by Titus, Jerusalem was overtaken by the Roman Army in A. D. 70 and the sufferings of the inhabitants of the City were so great that mothers cooked and ate their own children. Note that this is past. And verse 24 has been fulfilled for the Jews have been "**led away captive into ALL NATIONS,**" where they still remain, and Jerusalem has since then been "**TRODDEN DOWN OF THE GENTILES,**" and will continue to be until the "**TIMES OF THE GENTILES**" shall be fulfilled. But the "flight" that Matthew speaks about is still future. He locates it at the time of the "Great tribulation," which he says is to be preceded by the

setting up of the "ABOMINATION OF DESOLATION," spoken of by Daniel the Prophet. The heathen's idol gods are called "ABOMINATIONS." Milcom, or Molech, was the "**abomination**" of the Ammonites; Chemosh, the "abomination" of Moab (I. Kings 11: 5-7). This explains the "ABOMINATION" spoken of by Daniel, as nothing other than an "IDOL" OR "FALSE GOD." In the "middle of the week," a "DESOLATOR" (Antichrist) will appear and cause the sacrifices and oblations to cease, and set up in the "Holy Place" of the Temple an "**IDOL,**" AND THAT "Idol" will be an "IMAGE OF THE BEAST." (Rev. 13: 14-15).

When we look at the "Flight of the Woman" we can now locate "her place," the "chamber" to which she is to flee, and shut the door, and "hide herself for a little while," and be nourished by God for 3 ½ years. (Time, and Times, and Half a Time).

THE CITIES OF REFUGE.

The "Cities of Refuge" of Old Testament times are a type of this "Wilderness Refuge" of the Children of Israel, they were designated cities, 3 on each side of the river Jordan, where the "Man-Slayer" could flee for safety from the "Avenger of Blood." If it was proved after trial that he had slain a man "wilfully," he was turned over to the "Avenger of Blood," but if he did it unwittingly, his life was spared, but he had to remain in the city until the death of the High Priest. If there was no "Man-Slayer" there would be no "Avenger of Blood," and therefore no need for a "City of Refuge."

Now if we find in the New Testament that a certain class of people are called upon to flee to a "Place of Refuge" for the protection of their lives, then we must believe that they fled because an "Avenger of Blood" is after them, and that they fled because they were guilty of "Manslaughter."

Such a class of people can be found in the Jewish Race. They were the cause of the death of Christ, and though He was crucified by the Roman authorities they assumed the guilt for they cried---"**His blood be on us, and on Our Children**." (Matt. 27: 25). The Prayer of Jesus on the cross---"Father, forgive them for they know not what they do," make's it clear that Jesus' death was not so much a premeditated murder as it was a murder committed in a blind religious frenzy. Paul says in I. Cor. 2: 8,---"had they known they would not have crucified the Lord of Glory." Therefore, the Jewish race is only guilty of "Manslaughter." As the "Man-Slayer" of Jesus, they have been for over 2000 years looking for a "City of Refuge" and they have not as yet reached it. The "Avenger of Blood" has been on their track from nation to nation, and has followed them down thru the centuries, and the prophecy of Moses is being fulfilled that they should find no rest for the sole of their foot. (Deut. 28: 64-67).

If the Jews are the "Man-Slayer" who is the "Avenger of Blood"? Antichrist. And now as to the "City of Refuge" that God will provide for Israel when the "Avenger of Blood" who is the Antichrist, who shall then be indwelt by the Dragon, is on her track. The Prophet Daniel says, speaking of the Antichrist---"He shall enter also into the Glorious Land of Palestine and many countries shall be overthrown; but these shall **escape** out of his hand, even **Edom** and **Moab** and the chief of the **Children of Ammon**." (Dan. 11: 41).

Now Edom takes in the wilderness where Israel wandered for 40 years. And it is here in Edom that the "City of Refuge" that God has provided for Israel is located, and is known today as Petra. It was a great commercial centre in the days of King Solomon. In A. D. 105 the Romans conquered the country and called the province Arabia Petra. When the power of Rome declined Petra gradually fell into the hands of the Arabs and became completely lost to the civilized world in the seventh century, and remained so until it was rediscovered by Burckhardt in 1812.

When the time comes for the "Man-Slayer" (who is Israel), to escape from the hands of the "Avenger of Blood" (who is the Antichrist), the rocky fastness of the ancient City of Petra will be her "City of Refuge." When the "Woman" (Israel) shall flee into the Wilderness that the "Serpent" (Antichrist) shall cast a flood of water out of his mouth after her to destroy her, except that the earth shall open her mouth and swallow the flood. In other words, Antichrist will send his army after the fleeing Israelites, and it will probably be swallowed up in a "sand storm" of the desert, and Israel shall safely reach her place of refuge, where she shall be safe, not until the death of the High Priest, but until the return of "The High Priest" (Jesus) from Heaven, who as "King-Priest" of the armies of Heaven will deliver her and allow her to leave her place of refuge. During the period of Israel's "hiding" in the wilderness God will "nourish" her as He did during her 40 years' wandering in the same Wilderness in the days of Moses.

5. THE JEWISH REMNANT.
Rev. 12: 17.

Baffled in his attempt to destroy the "Woman," the Dragon, in his rage will make war against the "REMNANT OF HER SEED,"(the Woman) in other words, against those Israelites left in Palestine or among the nations that keep the "**Commandments of God,**" and have the "**testimony of Jesus Christ**." To this end he will give to the "**BEAST**" (Antichrist) his "Power," and his "**seat,**" and "**Great Authority**." Rev. 13: 2.

Here we have indirect evidence that the "Woman is not the Church, she is Israel. When the Church is caught out, no REMNANT is left behind, everyone that are "IN CHRIST" are taken away; but when the "woman" (ISRAEL) flees into the wilderness a "REMNANT" is left behind. This "Remnant" is composed of two classes. First, those who "**Keep the commandments of God,**" that is, Orthodox Jews who observe the Old Testament Law, and second, those who "**accept the testimony of Jesus Christ,**" Those that accept Jesus as their promised Messiah. The latter class will be converted by the preaching of the "Gospel of the Kingdom" by the "Two Witnesses." Those will be trying times for those Israelites who will not commit idolatry by bowing their knee to the "Image of the Beast," for it will be a remorseless war of persecution that Antichrist will wage against them, and thousands will die a martyr's death.

6. THE BEAST OUT OF THE SEA.

The Incarnation Of "The Dragon," "The Anti-God."

In "The Beast" Or "Anti-Christ." (Rev. 13: 1-10).

John next saw the "**Dragon**" standing on the seashore, and as he stood, a "Beast" rose up out of the sea having "SEVEN HEADS" and "TEN HORNS," and upon his "Horns" "TEN CROWNS," and upon his "Heads" the name of BLASPPHEMY, and the body of the "Beast" was like a LEOPARD, and his **feet** were as the feet of a BEAR, and his mouth as the mouth of a LION, and the "DRAGON" gave him his **POWER**, and his **SEAT** (Throne), and **GREAT AUTHORIT**. This does not necessarily mean that the "Dragon" gave him his own throne, but he gave him **power,** and a throne, and great authority. As John was back on the Isle of Patmos, the "sea from which he saw the "Beast" arise was probably the Mediterranean, though the "sea" in prophecy signifies the nations. We must go back to the book of Daniel's for an explanation of the symbol of the "BEAST." But before we take that up it is important to note that both the Old and New Testaments speak of a "**MYSTERIOUS AND TERRIBLE PERSONAGE**" who shall be revealed in the "Last Times." He is called by various names. Old Testament-- "The Assyrian." --- Isaiah 10: 5-6; 30: 27-33. "King of Babylon." ---Isaiah 14: 4. "Lucifer."--- Isaiah 14: 12. "The Little Horn." Daniel 7: 8; 8: 9-12. New Testament—"The Man of Sin." & "Son of Perdition." & "That Wicked." –II Thess. 2: 3-8. "Antichrist." I. John 2: 18. "The Beast."-- Rev. 13: 1-2.(Jesus also made a prophetic reference to him in John 5: 43).

Isaiah's Viewpoint.

The Prophet Isaiah sees the Antichrist as the "ASSYRIAN." Isa. 10: 5, 12, 24; 30: 27-33. In Isa. 11: 4, a chapter which is evidently Messsianic, we read that among other things which the Messiah will do—"He shall smite the earth with the 'rod of His mouth,' and with the 'breath of His lips' shall He slay '**THE WICKED**'." The word translated "**THE WICKED**," is singular and cannot refer to wicked persons in general, but to some **one person who is comspicuously wicked**. The expression appears to be like that of Paul's in II. Thess. 2: 8. "Then shall that '**WICKED**' be revealed, whom the Lord shall consume with the '**Spirit of His Mouth**,' and shall destroy with the '**Brightness of His Coming**'." It is evident that Isaiah and Paul are referring to the same person, who is undoubtly the Antichrist.

In Isa. 14: 4-17 there is a "**King of Babylon**" who shall smite the people in his wrath, and rule the nations in anger. He is called "**LUCIFER, Son of the Morning**," and he is cast down to Hell (or Sheol, the Underworld), where his coming creates a great stir among the Kings of the earth that have preceded him, and who says when they see him---"Art thou also become weak as we are? Art thou become like unto us? . . . Is this the man that made the earth to tremble, that did shake Kingdoms; that made the world as a wilderness and destroyed the cities thereof; that open not the house of his prisoners?" However, there has never as yet been such a King of Babylon as is described here; it must therefore refer to to some future King of Babylon, when Babylon shall be rebuilt. Verse 12-14 of Isa. Chapter 14 is evidently referring to Satan, and are descriptive of him before his fall, however, he is to incarnate himself in the Antichrist, who is to be a future King of Babylon, which would explains the source of the pride and presumption of Antichrist, which will lead to his downfall, as it did to Satan's.

DANIEL'S VIEWPOINT.

1. THE COLOSSUS.

The book of Daniel may be divided into two parts. The first six chapters are Historical, the last six are Prophetical. The baao contains one "Dream" by Nebucgadnezzar, and four "Visions" by Daniel, all relating to the "Times of the Gentiles." Nebuchadnezzar in his "Dream" saw a "**Great Image**" or "**COLOSSUS.**" The Head of the "Image" was of fine gold, its Breast and Arms of silver, its belly and thighs of brass, its legs of iron, and its Feet of iron and clay. This Image was destroyed by a "**Stone**" cut out of a mountain supernaturally. The "**Stone**" in turn became a **great mountain** and filled the **WHOLE EARTH.** (Dan. 2: 31—35).

The four metals of which the "**COLOSSUS**" was composed represented **Four Worldwide Empires** which were to arise in succession. (Dan. 2: 37-40). Four great Empires, and they were to succeed each other in the government of the world, from Nebuchadnezzar (B. C. 606) to the "Second Coming" of Christ---they were Babylonian, Medo-Persian, Grecian, and Roman. The First---"BABYLONIAN" is indicated by Daniel while interpreting the vision to Nebuchadnezzar. "**THOU** art this **Head of Gold.**" (Dan. 2: 38). The Second---the "**MEDO-PERSIAN,**" Daniel points out in his account of "Belshazzar's Feast," by the emphatic words---"In that night was Belshazzar the King of the Chaldeans slain, and Darius the **MEDIAN took the Kingdom**." (Dan. 5: 30-31). The Third---the "**GRECIAN,**" IS mentioned in (Dan. 8: 20-21), "the **Ram** which thou sawest having '**two horns**' are the Kings of Media and Persia, and the 'Rough Goat' is the King of Greece." The Fourth----the "ROMAN," is referred to in Dan. 9: 26 as--- "the **PEOPLE** of the '**Prince**' that should destroy the City of Jerusalem and the Sanctuary," now it is well known that it was the **ROMANS** under Titus, that destroyed Jerusalem in

A. D. 70. While these Four Great Empires were to follow each other in the order named, they were not to follow without a break. The Babylonian lasted from B. C. 606 to B. C. 538. The Medo-Persian from B. C. 538 to B. C. 330. The Grecian from B. C. 330 to B. C. 323. Then the Grecian was broken up into four parts, Thrace, Macedonia, Syria, and Egypt, and the last of these was conquered by the Romans in B. C. 30, and the Roman Empire lasted from B. C. 30 to A. D. 364, when it was divided into its Eastern and Western Divisions. Since then there has been no leading world Empire, and cannot be according to this prophecy until Christ sets up His "Millennial Kingdom," as represented by the "Stone" that smites the "COLOSSUS" on its feet, for this "STONE KINGDOM" is to fill the whole earth, and thus be universal. This "STONE" cannot be Christianity, for it does not fill the earth by degrees, and thus crowd out the "COLOSSUS," but it at one Blow DEMOLISHES IT. The action of the "STONE" is that of JUDGMENT not Grace, and is **SUDDEN** and **CALAMITOUS**. Now the time of the destruction is not until **after the formation of the Toes**, also the "TWO LIMBS" did not appear until A. D. 364, and the "**TEN TOES**" had not yet developed. We are told in Dan. 2: 44 that "in the days of **THOSE KINGS**" speaking of the Kings represented by the "**Ten Toes**," which corresponds with the "**Ten Horns**" of Daniel's "Fourth Wild Beast," (Dan. 7: 7-8), and with the "**Ten Kings**" of John's "**Beast**." (Rev. 17: 12). The first four Kingdom were literal Kingdoms, and so must the "**Stone Kingdom**" be, for it is to take the place of those Kingdoms, and fill the whole earth. It represents therefore the "Millennial Kingdom" of Christ, for He is the "STONE" of the Scripture. (Matt. 21: 44).

Therefore, the "**COLOSSUS**" of "Nebuchadnezzar's dream" symbolized the "World Kingdoms" in their Unity and Historical Succession. Gentile dominion is represented by a huge "**METALLIC MAN**." The degeneration of the "World Kingdoms" can be seen in the diminishing value of the metals used. Silver is worth less than gold, brass less than silver, iron less then brass, and clay less than iron. The weight of the "COLOSSUS" also declines; the specific gravity of gold was 19.5, of silver 10.47, of brass 8, of cast-iron 5, and of clay 1.93. The "**Colossus**" was **TOP HEAVY**. The character of the governing power also deteriorates from an "**Absolute Monarchy**" under Nebuchadnezzar, to an "**Autocratic Democracy**" symbolized by the mixture of the iron and clay of the feet. We have dwelt at length on the "Colossus," for it is only as we understand it, that we can understand the meaning of the "Wild Beasts" that Daniel saw come up out of the sea.

2. THE VISION OF THE "FOUR BEASTS."

Forty-eight years after Nebuchadnezzar had his "Dream," B. C. 555, Daniel in vision stood upon the shore of the Mediterranean Sea, and saw four "**Great Beasts**" come up out of the sea in succession.

FIRST BEAST: The "First Beast" was like a LION and had Eagle's Wings, and as the Prophet watched it, he saw it lifted up from the earth, and made to stand upon its feet as a **Man,** and a man's heart was given to it. Dan. 7: 4. In London you can visit the British Museum and examine the Colossal Stone Lion with the "**wings of an eagle**" and the "**head of a man,**" disinterred from the ruins of Babylon and Assyria by Sir Henry Layard between the years 1840 and 1850 A. D.,

SECOND BEAST: The "Second Beast" was "like to a **BEAR**, and it raised up itself on one side, and it had "**Three Ribs**" in the mouth of it, between the teeth of it: and they said unto it Arise, devour much flesh." (Dan. 7: 5). The bear is the strongest beast after the Lion and is distinguished for its voracity, but it has none of the agility and majesty of the Lion, is awkward in its movements, and effects its purpose with comparative slowness, and by brute force and sheer strength. These were the characteristics of the Medo-Pesian Empire. It was ponderous in its movements. It did not gain its victories by bravery or shill, but overwhelmed its enemies by hurling vast masses of troops upon them. The side of the "**BEAR**" which raised up to attack signifies Persia, in which lay the greatest military strength, and corresponded to the "right shoulder and arm" of the "**Colossus**." The "Three Ribs" stood for the three Kingdoms of **Lydia, Babylon** and **Egypt**, which formed a "**Triple Alliance**" to check the Medo-Persian power, but were all destroyed by it.

THIRD BEAST: The "Third Beast" was "like a LEOPARD, which had upon the back of it **four wings of a fowl;** the '**BEAS**T' had also **four heads**; and dominion was given to it." (Dan. 7: 6). The Leopard is the most agile and graceful of creatures; but its speed is here still further assisted by "wings." Slight in its frame, but strong, swift and fierce, its characteristics render it a fitting symbol of the rapid conquests of the Greeks under Alexander the Great, who followed by small but well-equipped and splendidly brave armies, moved with great celerity and in about 10 years overthrew the unwieldy forces of Persia, and subdued the whole civilized world.

The "**FOUR HEADS**" of the **LEOPARD** represent the "**Four Kingdoms**" into which the Empire of Alexander was divided by his generals, namely **Thrace**, **Macedonia**, **Syria** and **Egypt**. The "Third Beast" corresponds to the "**Abdomen**" and "Hips" of the "**COLOSSUS**."

FOURTH BEAST: The "Fourth Beast" was unlike any Beast that Daniel had ever seen or heard about. It was "dreadful and terrible, and strong exceedingly, and it had large **IRON TEETH**. It devoured and brake into pieces, and stamped the other Beasts with the feet of it; and it was diverse from all the other 'BEASTS' that were before it, and it had "TEN HORNS." (Dan. 7: 7). The fact that this Beast had "Iron Teeth," and that there were "Ten Horns" on its Head, caused Daniel to compare the "Iron" with the "Iron Limbs," and the "Ten Horns" to the "Ten Toes" of the "**COLOSSUS**," this caused Daniel to see that the "Fourth Beast" stood for the Fourth world Empire, the **Roman Empire**.

As Daniel Considered the "**Ten Horns**," he was amazed to see another "Horn," a LITTLE one, come up among them, and before whom there were "**three**" of the "**First Horns**" plucked up by the roots, that is destroyed. And as he examined the "**LITTLE HORN**" more closely he noticed that it had **Eyes** like the eyes of a **Man, and the Mouth of a Man** speaking great things. (Dan. 7: 8). This troubled Daniel. He had seen nothing corresponding to it on the "**Ten Toes**" of the "**COLOSSUS**." It must mean some new and additional revelation that God had not seen fit to impart to the Gentile King Nebuchadnezzar, and that was reserved for Daniel and his people (the Jews). Let us not forget that Daniel's own visions, in the last six chapters of the of the book(Daniel's), have to do with God's dealings with the **Jewish People** in the "**LATTER DAYS**." (Dan. 10: 14). So Daniel approached one of THE "Heavenly Messengers" that stood by and asked him the meaning of what he had seen. He was told that the "**Four Beasts**" stood for "**FOUR KINGS**" or "**KINGDOMS**" that should arise out of the earth. Then Danielnted to know the "truth" about the "**FOURTH Beast**," which was so diverse from the other three, and particularly about the "LITTLE HORN" that came up among the "Ten Horns" on its head. In explanation Daniel was told that the "Ten Horns" on the "Fourth Beast" represented "TEN KINGS" that shall arise, and that the "Little Horn" was a "King" that should rise among them and subdue three of them, and that he would be a "PERSON" of remarkable intelligence and great oratorical powers, having a mouth **speaking great things**. That he would be audacious, arrogant, imperious, and persecuting, and changing "**times and laws**," and that the "Saints of the Most High" (Daniel's People) would be given into his hands for 3 ½ years.

In this vision of the "Four Beasts" we see "**Degeneration**" just as we saw it in the metals of the "COLOSSUS." The descent is from the LION, the "King of Beasts," to a nondescript "MONSTER" that defies description. The reason why these "Four Kingdoms" are represented first as a "**Golden Headed Metallic Image**," and then as a succession of "**Wild Beasts**," was to show the difference between **Man's** view and **GOD'S** view of the World Kingdoms. Man sees in them the concentration of wealth, majesty and power; God sees them as a succession of rapacious Wild Beasts devouring one another.

3. THE VISION OF THE "RAM" AND THE "HE-GOAT."

The explanation as to the meaning of the "LITTLE HORN" perplexed Daniel, and he voiced it by saying "My 'cogitations' much troubled me, and my countenance changed in me; but I kept the matter in my heart." (Dan. 7: 28). Two years later God transported Daniel in vision to Shushan, the Capital of Persia, as a means of comforting him, and as he stood on the bank of the riverUlai, he saw a **RAM** which had **"Two Horns,"** one higher than the other, and the higher one came up last. And the Ram did according to its will. (Dan. 8: 4). While Daniel was "considering" what the Vision of the RAM meant, he saw a HE-GOAT come from the west unmolested, and he noticed it had a "NOTABLE HORN" between its eyes, and when it reached the RAM it was moved with anger against it, and smote it with "fury," and broke its "Two Horns," and knocked it down and stamped upon it. Then the HE-GOAT waxed great, but when it became strong its "GREAT HORN" was broken off, and "Four Notable Horns" came up in its place, and out of one of them spramg a "LITTLE HORN" which waxed exceedingly great toward the "South," and toward the "East," and toward the "Pleasant Land" (Palestine). (Dan. 8: 5-9). When Daniel sought for the Meaning of this Vision he heard a voice say—"Gabriel, make this man to understand the Vision." Then Gabriel said to Daniel the Vision belongs to the "**Time of the End**" (the End of the times of the Gentiles), and is to make thee know what shall come to pass in the "**Last End of the Indignation**" in other words "**The Great Tribulation**." (Dan. 8: 15-19).

Gabriel then informed Daniel that the "RAM" stood for the "Medo-Persian Empire," with its two Kings, Darius and his nephew Cyrus, and that the "HE-GOAT" stood for the "Grecian Empire," and the "GREAT HORN" between its eyes for its first King (Alexander the Great), and that the "FOUR HORNS" that took the place of the "GREAT HORN," stood for "Four Kingdoms" into which the "Grecian Empire" should be divided.

This explanation revealed to Daniel that the "TWO HORNS" of the RAM, one higher than the other, and the "TWO SHOULDERS" of the BEAR, one higher than the other, and the "TWO ARMS" of the COLOSSUS, stood for the same thing, the double Empire of Medo-Persia. Daniel also saw that the "FOUR HORNS" that came up in the place of the "GREAT HORN" represents the "FOUR HEADS" of the LEOPARD, and therefore must also represent the "ABDOMEN" and "HIPS" of the COLOSSUS, and stand for the Grecian Empire, and its "Fourfold Division" among the Generals of Alexander the Great. But Daniel was still troubled as to the meaning of the "LITTLE HORN" that he saw come out of the "Four Horns" of the **HE-GOAT**, and Gabriel told him that it stood for a King of "Fierce Countenance" who should stand up in the "**LATTER TIME**" of the Kingdom, and who should stand up against the "**PRINCE OF PRINCES**" (Christ). (Dan. 8: 23-25). The description of this "LITTLE HORN" clearly decribes the "LITTLE HORN" that Daniel saw arise amid the "Ten Horns" of the "Fourth Wild Beast," that he saw, and that it stood for the same person. The revelation so overcame Daniel that he "fainted," and was sick several days. (Dan. 8: 27).

I. PAUL'S VIEWPOINT.

In the American Standard Edition of the Bible the Antichrist is called the "MYSTERY OF LAWLESSNESS" or the "LAWLESSNESS ONE." AS such he is not the cause of Lawlessness, he is the result or fruit of it.

The name that the Apostle Paul gives the Antichrist, "**SON OF PERDITION**," is not without significance. It was first used by Christ of Judas (John 17: 12), and then here of **Antichrist**. The Apostle also calls the Antichrist in this passage the "**MYSTERY OF INIQUITY**." In I Tim. 3: 16 Christ is spoken of as the "**MYSTERY OF GODLINESS**," in other words He was God **MANIFEST IN THE FLESH**, by being born of the Virgin Mary by the Holy Spirit. Therefore Jesus became the **SON OF GOD.** (Luke 1: 35). Since iniquity is the opposite of godliness, then the "**MYSTERY OF INIQUITY**" must be the opposite of the "**MYSTERY OF GODLINESS**." And as Christ was the "Son of God," then Antichrist must be the "**SON OF PERDITION**," that is son of **SATAN**. And as Christ was born of a virgin by the Holy Spirit, so Antichrist will be born of a **woman** (not necessarily a virgin) by Satan. This is no new view for it has been held by many of God's spiritually minded people since the days of the Apostle John, and there is some warrant for it in the Scriptures. In Gen. 3; 15, God said to the Serpent (Satan), "I will put enmity between thee and the woman, and between "**THY SEED' AND 'HER SEED'**." Now the woman's **SEED** was **CHRIST**, then the Serpent's **SEED** must be **ANTICHRIST**. In John 8: 44 Jesus said to the Jews—"Ye are of your father **THE DEVIL**. . . . . When he speaketh a lie, he speaketh of his own; for he is a liar, and the father of **IT**." In the Greek, there is the definite article before "**lie**," and it should read "**THE LIE**," so when the Devil speaks of "**THE LIE**," he is speaking of his own (child), for he is a liar, and the **FATHER OF "IT"---"THE LIE."** And it is worthy of note that in verse 11, that follows the passage we are considering that the Apostle says---"And for this cause God shall send them strong delusion that they should believe **a lie.**" Here again the definite article is found in the Greek, and it should read "**THE LIE,**" the "**SON OF PERDITION,**" the **ANTICHRIST**.

That being said, why was Judas called the "**SON OF PERDITION**"? Was he a child of Satan by some woman, or was he simply indwelt by Satan? Let's let the Scriptures speak for themselves. In John 6: 70-71 we read that Jesus said "Have not I chosen you twelve, and one of you is a **DEVIL**? He spake of Judas Iscariot the son of Simon; for he it was that should betray Him, being one of the Twelve." In no other passage than this is the word "Devil" applied to anyone but to Satan himself. Here the Greek word is "**diabolus,**" the definite article is employed, and it should read---"and one of you is **THE DEVIL.**" This would make judas the Devil **incarnate**, or the "**MYSTERY OF INIQUITY,**" and explains why Jesus in John 17: 12, calls him the "**SON OF PERDITION.**"

This is the only place in the Scriptures where the word "**diabolus**" is applied to a human being, and it implies an incarnation. While "**perdition**" is a **PLACE** (Rev. 17: 8, 11), it is also a "**condition**" into which men fall (I. Tim. 6: 9; Heb. 10: 39), and while men who have committed the "Unpardonable Sin" are "**sons of perdition,**" because they are destined to the place of the irrevocably lost, yet Judas and Antichrist are the "**SONS OF PERDITION**" in a special sense, for they are the **SONS** of "**Perdition**"---**THE DEVIL**. Which means that they are not merely "obsessed" or controlled by the Devil, but the Devil has incarnated himself in them, and for the time being, for all practical purposes, they are the very Devil himself.

The next question that arises is, "If Judas and the Antichrist are both called the '**SON OF PERDITION,**' are they one and the same, or are there **two 'Sons of Perdition'?**" Here we must anticipate. In Rev. 11: 7, we read that the "Beast" that slays the "Two Witnesses" ascends out of the "**Bottomless Pit**"

(ABYSS), and that "Beast" is the ANTICHRIST. Now how did he get into the "**ABYSS**"? Well, if there is only one "**SON OF PERDITION**," and Judas and Antichrist are one and the same, then he got in the **ABYSS** when Judas went to his "**Own Place**" (the **ABYSS**). (Acts 1: 25). Of no other person is it said anywhere in the Scriptures that he went "**to his own place.**" Now we look again in Rev. 17: 8 and it is said---"The '**Beast**' that thou sawest **was**, and is **not**: and shall **ascend out of the Bottomless Pit**' (ABYSS), and go into **PERDITION.**" As this "Beast" is the same that slays the "**Two Witnesses**" he is the **ANTICHRIST**.

The question then arises, when was "**Antichrist**" on the earth before? If Judas and Antichrist are one and the same the enigma is solved. When Judas was on earth he **WAS**; when Judas went to his "**Own place**" he "**WAS NOT**"; When Judas comes back from the "**Abyss**" he will be---**THE ANTICHRIST**.

II. JOHN'S VIEWPOINT.

When we compare these "Foreviews," and note the similarity of conduct of Daniel's "**LITTLE HORN**," Paul's "MAN OF SIN," and John's "BEAST" we see that they are to continue for the same length of time---3 ½ years, and that Daniel's "LITTLE HORN" and Paul's "MAN OF SIN," and John's "BEAST," are all to be destroyed in the same manner at **Christ's "second Coming**,"

Before we examine in detail John's "BEAST," it would be well for to compare it with Daniel's "**FOURTH WILD BEAST**." Now in comparing these two "BEASTS" we find that they both came up out of the sea (the nations), and they are utterly unlike any beast we have ever heard of. Daniel's "Beast's" was dreadful and terrible, and strong exceedingly; and it had great iron teeth, and nails of brass; while John's "Beast" was like a LEOPARD, with the feet of a bear, and the mouth of a **LION**. Since Daniel's "Beast" represented the "**FOURTH KINGDOM**" upon the earth, which is the Roman Empire, it is evident that its characteristics describe the old Roman Empire, while the characteristics of John's Beast represent the revived Roman Empire. Now the Old Roman Empire was "strong exceedingly" and its grip and power were like a beast with "**great iron teeth**" and "**nails of brass**," and from the description of John's "Beast" the revived Roman Empire shall embody all the characteristics of the Four World Empires, as seen in its **LEOPARD** like body, its feet of a **BEAR**, and its mouth of a **LION**. because both "Beasts" have **TEN HORNS** reveals that they will be in existence at the time indicated by the **TEN TOES** of the colossus, with which they correspond, which will be just before the setting up of the Millennial Kingdom of Christ. Now we are told that the "**TEN HORNS**" of Daniel's "**Beast**" stand for "**TEN KINGS**," and the "**TEN HORNS**" of John's "Beast" stand for the same. (Rev. 17: 12). Thus Daniel and John foresaw that the Roman Empire was to be eventually divided into "Ten Separate but Federated Kingdoms."

While both "Beasts" have **TEN HORNS**, they differ in that John's had "**SEVEN HEADS**" while Daniel's had but **ONE HEAD**, and among the "**TEN HORNS**" on Daniel's "**Beast**" there came up a "**LITTLE HORN**," which is not seen within the "**TEN HORNS**" of John's Beast. We shall see that these are features that refers to the last stage of the "Beast" and show that we cannot understand the last stage of the "Beast" without carefully comparing Daniel's and John's "Beasts," for the "LITTLE HORN" OF Daniel's "Beast" plucks up **THREE** of the "**TEN HORNS**" of John's "Beast" and destroys them, or takes their Kingdom away, John left this out. The Antichristian character of Daniel's "**Beast**" is seen in its "**LITTLE HORN**" whose conduct corresponds with the whole of John's "Beast," and that for the same length of time, which equals "**FORTY AND TWO MONTHS**," **or 3 ½ years**.

Let us now analyze the "Beast" that John saw come up out of the sea, and try to figure out the meaning of its various members. There are two descriptions of this "**Beast**." Daniel's "Fourth Wild Beast" represented the Roman Empire as it existed from B. C. 30, until as a nation it shall cease to exist. This "Beast" was divided in A. D. 364, as the result of an ecclesiastical schism, into its Eastern and Western Divisions, and lost its national life as a world power, yet it has never lost its religious existence or influence as seen in the continuance of the Greek and Roman Churches; and Roman Law is still a controlling power in our laws. In this sense the Roman Empire in its influence has never ceased to exist. We can now consider it in its last stage as outlined in John's "Beast."

In the two descriptions of John's Beast as given above it is very important to see that the "Beast" has a "Dual" meaning. It represents both the revived Roman Empire, and its Imperial Head, the Antichrist. As the revived Roman Empire it is seen coming up out of the sea of the nations, as the Antichrist it comes up out of the **ABYSS**. It cannot be said of the Roman Empire of John's day, that it **WAS** and **WAS NOT**, for the Roman Empire was at the height of its power in John's day. Neither can it be said that---"it shall ascend out of the pit and go into **PERDITION**," for that could only be said of **a person**. Again we must distinguish between the body of the "Beast" and its **heads** and **horns**. The body being that of a **LEOPARD**, with the feet of a **BEAR**, and the mouth of a **LION** is to show that the revived Roman Empire in its last stage will include the characteristics of the first "Three Wild Beasts" of Daniel, that is, of the **LION** (Babylon), the **BEAR** (Medo-Persia), and the **LEOPARD** (Greece), and as the largest part of the "Beast," the Body, is represented by the **LEOPARD**, the prevailing characteristic of the revived Roman Empire will be **GRECIAN**.

The "Beast" that comes up out of the sea In Chapter 13, has SEVEN HEADS and TEN HORNS, and the "Horns" are CROWNED. This represents the Empire, at the height of its power, when it will have all its "**Heads**," and when the heads of the **TEN KINGDOMS** into which the Empire shall be divided, will have been crowned. The "Beast" that comes up out of the ABYSS also has SEVEN HEADS and TEN HORNS, but they are not crowned, for the TEN KINGS represented by the TEN HORNS, have not as yet received their Kingdom. (Rev. 17: 12.) This implies that the "Beast" of Rev. 17, represents the Antichrist at the beginning of the "week." The "Scarlet Clothed Woman" is not seen until Chapter 17, however, it is clear that she rides the "Beast" from the beginning of the "week," for she represents the "**PAPAL CHURCH**" that comes into power after the true Church has been caught out. During the wars preceding the rise of Antichrist, the nations that will then be found in the geographical limits of the Old Roman Empire will form an "Alliance" for mutual protection. Those nations will be ten in number, represented by the "TEN HORNS" of the Beast. The "Papal Church" will no doubt play a prominent part in those proceedings. Her reward will be restoration of political power, and this union of Church and State, in which the Church will have control, is shown by the **WOMAN** riding the **Beast**, thus dominating it. But when the "Ten Kings" shall receive their Kingdoms and be **CROWNED**, they "shall hate the WHORE, and shall make her **desolate** and **naked**, and shall eat her flesh, and burn her with fire." (Rev. 17: 16). Now the King that was on the throne in John's day was Domitian, who had banished John to the Isle of Patmos. The last or "SEVENTH KING" who is yet to come is undoubtedly the ANTICHRIST. Rev. 13: 3, tells us that one of the "SEVEN HEADS," or "KINGS," received a deadly wound. Which one is not stated. The inference is that it is the last, for the Beast has all of his "HEADS" before one of them is wounded. In Rev. 17: 11 he is called the Beast that WAS, and IS NOT, even he is the "EIGHTH," and is of the "SEVENTH," and goeth into PERDITION. The only clear explanation of this passage is that the "SEVENTH HEAD"---THE ANTICHRIST, is the one who receives the "**deadly wound**," probably at the hand of an assassin, and as his body is lying in state prepared for burial, he rises from the dead (Rev. 17: 14), and thus becomes the "EIGHTH," though he is of the "SEVENTH." By this resurrection of the Antichrist, Satann imitates the Resurrection of Christ and makes the world "**wonder after the Beast**" (Rev. 13: 3), and this add to his prestige and power. If this happen at the "Middle of the week," at the time the dragon is cast ot of heaven, it will account for the great change that takes place in the Antichrist, for before receiving his "deadly wound" he will be sweet and lovable, but after his resurrection or recovery he will become Devilish, the result of the Dragon incarnating himself in him. It is at this time that he breaks the covenant with the Jews and desecrates the Temple by setting up the "Abomination of Desolation" which is actual an "Idol Image" of himself--- The "DESOLATOR" who is the "LITTLE HORN" OF Daniel's "Fourth Wild Beast" will destroy three of the "Ten Kings" and firmly establish himself in the place of power, and as he does not appear as the "LITTLE HORN" until after the "TEN HORNS," known as the "Ten Federated Kingdoms," come into existence, it is clear that the Antichrist does not form the Federation, but is the outgrowth of it.

He will be as a "composite" man. One who has the abilities and powers of Nebuchadnezzar, Xerxes, Alexander the Great and Caesar Augustus. He will have the gift of attracting unregenerate men, and the irresistible fascination of his personality, his versatile attainments, superhuman wisdom, great administrative and executive ability, along with his powers as a consummate flatterer, a brilliant diplomatist, a superb statagist, will make him the most conspicuous and prominent of men. Know that all these gifts will be conferred on him by Satan, and he will be Satan's tool, to use as he chooses, for Satan will make of him a **SUPERMAN**.

He will pose as a great humanitarian, the friend of men, and the special friend of the Jewish race, and he will persuade them that he has come to usher in the "Golden Age" as was given by the prophets, and they will receive him as their Messiah. He will intoxicate men with a strong delusion and his never varying success. And when he shall be slain and rise again he will have lost none of these powers, but will be in addition the embodiment of all kinds of wickedness and blasphemy.

This Satan's Superman "shall wear out the saint's of the Most High, and think to change times and laws: and they shall be given into his hand until a time and times and the dividing of time." or 3 ½ years. (Dan. 7: 25). "He shall also stand up against the **'Prince of Princes**' (**Jesus**)." (Dan. 8: 25).

"He shall do according to his will: and he shall exalt himself and magnify himself above every god, and shall speak marvelious things against the God of Gods." (Dan. 11: 36).

"Who opposeth and exalteth himself above all that is called God, or that is worshipped; so that he **AS GOD** sitteth in the Temple of God (at Jerusalem) showing himself that he

IS GOD . . . whose coming is after the **Working of Satan** with all **power** and **Signs** and **Lying Wonders**." (IIThess. 2: 3-9).

BE IT KNOWN: There has never as yet appeared on this earth a person who answers the description given in the above Scriptures. Such a character is inconceivable. No writer would have invented such a character.

1. THE BEAST OUT OF THE EARTH.

The "False Prophet" Or "Anti-Spirit." (Rev. 13: 11-18)

After the Apostle John had seen and described the "Beast" that came up **out of the SEA**, he saw another "Beast" come up out of the **EARTH**. This "Second Beast," even though John does not say it was a Lamb; had "Two Horns" like a lamb. Because of this resemblance many claim that the "Second Beast" is the Antichrist, for Antichrist is suppose to imitate Christ. While the **LAMB** (Christ) is mentioned in the Book of Revelation 22 times, the description given of Him in chapter 5: 6, is that of a lamb having "**SEVEN HORNS**" not just "TWO." This differentiates Him from the "lamb-like Beast" that comes up out of the earth, though he is "lamb-like in appearance **SPEAKS AS A DRAGON**."

The "Second Beast" has a name. He is called the "**FALSE PROPHET**" three times. First in chapter 16: 13, then in chapter 19: 20, and again in chapter 20: 10. Twice he is associated with the "First Beast" (Antichrist) and once with the "Dragon" (Satan) and the "First Beast," and as they are **PERSONS** so must he be. The fact that he is called the "False Prophet" is proof that he is not the "Antichrist." Jesus said in Matt. 24: 24 that "There shall arise '**False Christs**' and '**False Prophets**,' and they shall show **Great Signs and Wonders**: insomuch that, if it were possible they shall deceive the very elect." Here Jesus differentiates between "FALSE CHRISTS" and "FALSE PROPHETS," therefore the "ANTICHRIST" and the "FALSE PROPHET" cannot be the same.

In the "Dragon," the "Beast," and the "False Prophet," we have the "**SATANIC TRINITY**," at least it's Satan's imitation of the "Divine Trinnity." In the unseen and invisible "Dragon" we have the **FATHER** (The **ANTI-GOD**). In the "Beast" we

117

have the "**SON OF PERDITION**" (the **ANTI-CHRIST**), begotten of the Dragon, who appears on the earth, dies, and is resurrected, and to whom is given a throne by his Father the Dragon. In the "False Prophet" we have the "**ANTI-SPIRIT**," who proceeds from the "Dragon Father" and "Dragon Son," and whose speech is like the Dragon's. Then The "Dragon" will be the "ANTI-GOD," the "Beast" the "ANTI-CHRIST," and the "False Prophet" the "ANTI-SPIRIT," and the fact that all three are cast ALIVE into the "Lake of Fire" (Rev. 20: 10) is proof that they together form a "Triumvirate" which we may well call---"**THE SATANIC TRINITY**."

Again the "Antichrist" is to be a **KING and rule over a KINGDOM.** He will accept the "Kingdoms of this world" that Satan offered Christ, and that Christ refused (Matt. 4: 8-10). He will **EXALT** himself and claim to be God. (II Thess. 2: 4). But the "False Prophet" is not a King, He does not exalt himself, he exalts the "First Beast" (Antichrist). His relation to the "First Beast" is the same as the Holy Spirit's relation to Christ. The "False Prophet" causeth the earth and them which dwell therein to worship the "First Beast." He also have power to give life, and in this he imitates the Holy Spirit. And as the followers of Christ are sealed by the Holy Spirit until the "**Day of Redemption**" (Eph. 4: 30); so, the followers of Antichrist shall be sealed by the False Prophet until the "Day of Perdition." (Rev. 13: 16-17).

Satan will then energize the False Prophet, that he can do this is clear, because Job 1: 16 states that "Satan secured permission from God to touch all that Job had, brought down "fire from heaven" and burned up Job's sheep and servants. The False Prophet then commands the people to make an "**IMAGE OF THE BEAST**." This is further proof that the "First Beast" is the Antichrist. It is a strange weakness of mankind that they must have some **VISIBLE** God to worship, and when the Children of Israel, who had been delivered from Egypt under Moses' leadership, thought he had forsaken them because he did not come down from the Mount, they called

Aaron to make them gods which should go before them, and Aaron made for them the "**GOLDEN CALF**." (EX. 32: 1-6). So the False Prophet will have the people make for the purpose of worship an "**IMAGE OF THE BEAST**." But the wonderful thing about the "**IMAGE**" is that the False Prophet will have power to give **LIFE** to it, and cause it to **SPEAK**, and to demand that all who will not worship it shall be put to death.

This "Image" reminds us of the "**GOLDEN IMAGE**" that Nebuchadnezzar commanded to be made and set up in the "Plain of Dura," in the province of Babylon (Dan. 3: 1-30), before which, at the sounding of musical instruments, the people were commanded to bow down and worship under penalty, for those who disobeyed, of being cast into a "**BURNING FIERY FURNACE**." Doubtless there will be many in the "Day of Antichrist" who will refuse to bow down and worship the "**Image of the Beast**," and who will not escape as did the "Three Hebrew Children," though God may interpose in a miraculous way to deliver some. And as if this was not enough, the False Prophet shall cause---"ALL, both small and great, rich and poor, free and bond, to receive a '**MARK**' in their **RIGHT HAND**, or in their **FOREHEAD**; and that no man might BUY or SELL, save he that has the 'MARK' or the NAME OF THE BEAST,' or the 'NUMBER OF HIS NAME.'" This "MARK" will be known as the "**BRAND OF HELL**."

This is what the world is fastly coming to. The time is not far away when the various "Trusts" and "Combinations of Capital" will be merged into a "FEDERATION OF TRUSTS," at the head of which shall be a "NAPOLEON OF CAPITAL." Ultimately this "Federation of Trusts" will extend to the whole world; at the head of which shall be **THE ANTICHRIST**, and the producer and consumer will be powerless in the tentacles of this **OCTOPUS**, and no man shall be able to buy or sell who has not the "**MARK OF THE BEAST**." This "MARK" will be **Branded** or burnt on. It will probably be the "**NUMBER OF THE BEAST**" or "666." The number "666" is the "**NUMBER OF MAN**," and stops short of the perfect number **SEVEN**.

In that day men will doubtless prefer to have the "MARK" on the back of their right hand so it can be readily seen in the act of signing checks, drafts, and receipts. There will doubtless be public officials in all public places of business to see that no one buys or sells who has not the "MARK." This will apply to women as well as men. No one can shop, or even buy from the huckster at the door, without the "MARK," **UNDER PENALTY OF DEATH**. What horriable times for those who will not WORSHIP THE BEAST; if they can neither buy or sell without the "MARK," for then they must beg, or starve or be killed. However, it doesn't end their; the doom of the "Satanic Trinity" will be, that at the close of that awful time of Tribulation the **LORD JESUS CHRIST** will return, and the "Dragon," and the "**Anti-God**," will be cast into the "**BOTTOMLESS PIT**" for a 1000 years (Rev. 20: 1-3), and the "Beast," the "**Anti-Christ**," and the "**False Prophet**," the "**Anti-Spirit**," will be cast **ALIVE** into the "**LAKE OF FIRE**."

THE INTERVAL BETWEEN THE "SEVEN PERSONAGES" AND THE "SEVEN VIALS."

1. THE LAMB ON MOUNT ZION. (REV. 14: 1-5.)

The Lamb here is Jesus Christ, and the Mount Zion is not Mount Zion of the earthly Jerusalem but of the Heavenly of which Paul speaks in Heb. 12: 22-23. "But ye are come unto Mount Zion, and unto the city of the living God, "THE HEAVENLY JERUSALEM,' and to an innumerable company of angels, to the general Asssembly and Church of the 'First Born' (New Born), which are written in Heaven, and to God the judge of all, and to the spirits of "**JUST**" men made perfect."

The 144,000 standing with the Lamb on Mount Zion, are the 144,000 "**SEALED ONES**," 12,000 from each of the Tribes of Israel. We are told in Rev. 7: 3-8 that they were sealed, here we are told why. In chapter seven we are told they were sealed in their foreheads, here we are told that, that sealing was the writing on their foreheads of the name of the Lamb and of the Lamb's Father. As John looked at the Lamb and the 144,000 "**Sealed Ones**" who stood with Him, he heard a voice from Heaven, as the voice of many waters, and as the voice of a "**great thunder**," who spoke with the voice of the speaker who spoke from the midst, of the "Lamp-stands" of chapter 1: 10, 15, or the Lamb Himself.

We are not told what the voice said, but it was followed with the voice or singing of "**Harpers**" accompanied by their harps. These "**Harpers**" sung a NEW SONG" before the Throne, and the "Four Living Creatures," and the "Elders." As the "Elders" represents the Church, these "Harpers" are not the Church, for they sing before the "Elders." We believe these "**Harpers**" to be those who stood on the "Sea of Glass" before the Throne in Rev. 4: 6. The "New Song" they sing is a "**double song**," the "**SONG OF MOSES**" and the "**SONG OF THE LAMB**," it was also said that no man could learn the songs but the 144,000 who were redeemed from the earth. This is also evidence that the 144,000 "Sealed Ones" are in Heaven, either having been translated or died a Marty's death, and from Rev. 14: 4 we are told that they are the "**First-Fruits**" of the restored nation of Israel.

These 144,000 "Sealed Ones" are called "VIRGINS"; and the fact that they are spoken of as not having been "**defiled with women**," shows that they are either all men of the character of the Apostle Paul, who did not marry, or as is most likely, and as the word translated "virgins" means person of either sex, they are "virgins" in the sense that they kept themselves clean of the crowning sin of that day **FORNICATION**, for the crowning sin of the Tribulation Period will be **fornication** (Rev. 9: 21; 14: 8), or looseness and laxity of the marriage tie, of which "free-love," and the doctrine of "affinities," and multiplied divorce in these days are but the opening wedge to the looseness of morals of those Anti-Christian times. The **144,000 "Sealed Ones"** will be especially delivered from this sin, and so they, and they only, as a special class, can sing this "New Song" of redemption, not so much by the blood, as from the sin of fornication. The teaching of "seducing spirits" mentioned in I Tim. 4: 1-3, as belonging to those Anti-Christian times, of "forbidding to marry and commanding to abstain from meats," has a deeper significance than that of the practice of the Church of Rome that requires the celibacy of the priesthood and clergy, and fasting of the laity. Such teaching comes from the "Pit," and belongs to Antichrist's religion, and its purpose is to weaken the body by fasting and make it more susceptible to the influence of evil angels and demons, and to cause it to gratify the desires of the flesh in other ways than by lawful means. These "Sealed Ones" are a chosen class who follow the Lamb whithersoever He goeth, and they are without fault before the Throne of God.

2. THE THREE ANGEL MESSENGERS.
FIRST ANGEL.

THE EVERLASTING GOSPEL. (REV. 14: 6-7).

In his vision of Apocalyptic Judgments John sees many angels at work. He sees one flying in "**MID-HEAVEN**." In other words, in the heaven or atmosphere that surrounds our earth. This Angel has a mission, which is to preach the "**EVERLASTING GOSPEL**" unto every nation, kindred, tongue, and people on the earth. This is the first and only place in the Bible where an **angel** is commissioned to preach the Gospel. An angel could not tell Cornelius how to be saved, he could only tell him to send for Peter for that purpose. (Acts 10: 3-6). In this "Gospel Age" only redeemed men can preach the Gospel, but at the "End Time," just before the return of the Lord, an angel will go forth to preach the "EVERLASTING GOSPEL," or as the revised version of the Bible puts it, the "**ETERNAL GOSPEL**." The word "Gospel" means "**Good News**." There are four forms of the Gospel mentioned in the New Testament, and we must distinguish carefully between them.

(1). THE GOSPEL OF "THE KINGDOM." (MATT. 24: 14).

This is the "Good News" that God purposes to set up a Kingdom on this earth over which David's Son, JESUS, shall reign, as prophesied in Luke 1: 32-33. Two preachings of this Gospel are mentioned, one past, beginning with the ministry of John the Baptist, and preached by Jesus and His Disciples, but it ended with the rejection of Jesus as King. This Gospel is to be preached again after the Church is taken out. It will be the fulfilment of Matt. 24: 14, where it says: "This Gospel of 'THE KINGDOM' shall be preached in all the world for a WITNESS unto all nations: and then shall the end come." This has no reference to the Gospel that has been preached to the nations. It is the Gospel of SALVATION, but

123

the "Gospel of the Kingdom" was not for "Salvation" but for a WITNESS, that is. It is the **announcement that the time has come to SET UP THE KINGDOM.** It will be preached first by Elijah the forerunner (Mal. 4: 5-6), and by others who shall be commissioned to bear the news to all nations as a proclamation of the Coming of Christ as King to occupy the Throne of David, and for the purpose of regathering Israel to the Promised Land.

(2). THE GOSPEL OF THE "GRACE OF GOD." (ACTS 20: 24).

This is the "Good News" that Jesus Christ the rejected King died on the Cross for our **SALVATION**. This form of the Gospel is described in many ways. It is called the "**GOSPEL OF GOD**" (Rom. 1: 1), because it has it source in the **LOVE OF GOD**. John 3: 16. Its **Character** is "**GRACE.**" Acts 20: 24. Its subject is **CHRIST** (Rom. 1: 16; IICor. 10: 14), and it is the **POWER OF GOD UNTIL SALVATION**. It is also a "**GLORIOUS GOSPEL**" because it speaks of Him who is in the **GLORY**, and has been **GLORIFIED**, and who is bringing many sons to **GLORY**. (I Tim. 1: 11, II Cor. 4: 4, Heb. 2: 10). And it is the "**GOSPEL OF PEACE**," because it makes peace between the sinner and God, and brings peace to the soul. (Eph. 6: 15).

(3). MY GOSPEL. (ROM. 2: 16; ACTS 26: 16-18).

This is the same as the "Gospel of the Grace of God," or of Salvation, with the additional revelations that were made known to Paul as to the Church (Eph. 3: 1-7), and as to Israel. Rom. 11: 1-36.

(4). THE "EVERLASTING GOSPEL." (REV. 14: 6).

This is what the Angel preaches in this chapter. It is neither the "Gospel of the Kingdom," nor of "Grace." Its burden is not Salvation but **JUDGMENT**. "Fear God, and give glory to Him: For the **HOUR OF HIS JUDGMENT IS COME**." It is "Good News" to Israel, and all who are passing through the "fires of judgement," because it declares that their troubles will soon end in the judgment and destruction of Antichrist. It calls on men to worship God as "Creator," and not as "Saviour," and so it is called in the Revised Version of the Bible---"**THE ETERNAL GOSPEL**," the Gospel that has been proclaimed from Eden down by Patriarchs and Prophets, and not an "Everlasting Gospel" in the sense that it saves men for all eternity.

There is "another Gospel" (Gal. 1: 6-12, IICor. 11: 4), which is not another, and which Paul repudiated. It is a perversion of the true Gospel and has many seductive forms, and in the main teaches that "faith is not **sufficient for Salvation**, nor able to keep and perfect you, and so emphasizes "Good Works." (Col. 2: 18-23, Heb. 6: 1, 9: 14). The Apostle pronounces a fearful "Anathema" upon its preachers and teachers. (Gal. 1: 8-9). Our message is: "**Believe on the Lord Jesus Christ and thou shalt be saved**." (Acts 16: 31). The Angel's message is "**Fear God for the Hour of His Judgement is come**." Men reject the human messenger and they will also reject the Angelic messenger, they will not believe even though ONE (Jesus) rose from the dead.

SECOND ANGEL.

FALL OF BABYLON PROCLAIMED. (REV. 14: 8).

Here is proof that the City of Babylon is to be rebuilt. For further proof see Rev. Chapter 18. As to the fall and destruction of the literal City of Babylon this proclamation is anticipative, but a a declaration that Babylon has fallen to fearful depths of wickedness and apostasy, and had become "**the habitation of demons, and the hold of every foul spirit, and a cage of every unclean and hateful bird**," as described in Rev. chapter 18: 2, it was already true, for the City of Babylon will have been rebuilt at the time when this Angel utters his proclamation. The Angel's warning was that God's people might hear His voice saying: "Come out of her, MY PEOPLE, that ye be not partakers of her sins, and that ye receive not of her plagues." (Rev. 18: 4).

THIRD ANGEL.

THE DOOM OF ANTICHRIST'S FOLLOWERS. (REV. 14: 9-11).

If it were possiable; we could say that **"God is really angry now"**. For this is a most awful warning; listen to this Angel as he says, "Any man who worships the Beast, and receive his 'Mark' in his forehead or hand, his doom is fixed **FOREVER**, and he shall be tormented with fire and brimstone in the presence of the Holy Angels and of the Lamb, and the smoke of his torment shall ascend for ever and ever, and they shall have no rest day or night." That means during the 3 ½ years of Antichrist's reign, after they have received the "Mark," for there is no day or night in eternity. If "Eternal Punishment" is not taught anywhere else in the Bible, it is taught here. Just think of the horror of remorse in the "Lake of Fire," as these worshippers of the Beast shall recall the "Mark of the Beast" as it was imprinted on their forehead or right hand with their own consent because of their desire to enrich themselves in the markets of their day.

1. THE BLESSED DEAD. (REV. 14: 12-13).

This is true of all saints but here it refers to those who die after the False Prophet has issued the command that all who will not worship the "Image of the Beast" "**shall be killed.**" (Rev. 13: 15). This warning is given for the benefit of those who in that day shall be tempted to compromise with evil in order to preserve their lives. The Scripture in Rev. 14: 13 uses the word **HENCEFORTH**, it's better to live and rein with Christ **1000 years,** than with Antichrist **3 ½ years**. This special class of dead who "DIE IN THE LORD" will be blessed because they will be delivered from the trials and sufferings of the Great Tribulation, and will receive the "**MARTYR'S CROWN**" (Rev. 2: 10), and they shall rest from their labors of stemming the tide of iniquity of those days, and their works follow with them. During the "Great Tribulation" they that are loyal to God have no prospect before them but martyrdom, thus, the need at this particular time of a special message of blessing to those who are faithful **until death**. What a contrast between the "Blessed Dead," and those who have the "Mark of the Beast." The former will rest from their labors, while the latter shall not rest day or night.

2. THE HARVEST AND VINTAGE. (REV. 14: 14-20).

There can be no question as to who is the "Rreaper" of the **HARVEST OF THE EARTH**." It is Jesus Christ Himself. He was the "Sower" and He shall be the "Reaper." Be it known that this is the "Harvest" of the Gentile Nations. Joel 3: 9-17 gives us a description of this "Harvest and Vintage." This "Harvest and Vintage" are **JUDICIAL**. Which means, they are for the purpose of Judgment. This account is anticipated. It looks forward to chapter 16: 13-16, which speaks of how the armies of the world are to be gathered together by "**THREE UNCLEAN SPIRITS**" to the battle of the great Day of God Almighty at Armageddon. This Battle takes place after the "Fall of Babylon," and is more fully described in chapter 19: 17-19.

We are told that the Harvest is **RIPE**, and the "Son of Man" is commanded to thrust in His Sickle, which He does, and while the pouring out of the "Vials" is a part of the reaping, the Harvest is not finished until the end of the "Battle of Amageddon." The difference between the "Harvest and the Vintage" is that the "harvest" in the natural world precedes the "vintage," but often, as in this case, continues until they become one.

The "Vintage" is of the "**VINE OF THE EARTH**." Israel was a "VINE" brought out of Egypt (Psa. 80: 8) and planted in Canaan, but when God looked for it to bring forth "**good grapes**" it brought forth "**WILD GRAPES**" (Isa. 5: 1-7), and fruit unto itself. (Hosea 10: 1) When the Lord of the "vineyard" sent His servants for the "Fruit of the Vineyard," the husbandmen beat one, killed another, and stoned yet another. At last He sent His Son, Him they took and cast out of the Vineyard and slew. (Matt. 21: 33-34). Then Jesus Himself became the "**TRUE VINE**," of which His disciples are the branches. (John 15: 5). The "**VINE OF THE EARTH**" is Antichrist and all who belong to his pernicious system.

The "**WINEPRESS**" is the winepress of the "**FIERCENESS AND WRATH OF ALMIGHTY GOD.**" (Rev. 19: 15). The Prophet Isaiah describes Christ's share in it in Isa. 63: 1-6. It will cover the whole land of Palestine, and extend as far south as Edom and Bozrah. So great shall be the slaugher that the blood shall be up to the horses bridles in the valleys over the whole of Palestine for 1600 furlongs, or 200 miles. This will be the time when the Prophet Isaiah speaks of, when the land shall be **DRUNK WITH BLOOD**. (Isa. 34: 7-8).

THE SEVEN LAST PLAGUES
OR VIAL JUDGMENTS.

(Rev. 15: 1).

This is a great and marvelous "**SIGN**" or "**WONDER**" because it completed the pouring out of the accumulated "**WRATH OF GOD.**"

PRELUDE.

THE SEA OF GLASS.

(Rev. 15: 2-4).

This "SEA OF GLASS' is the same "Sea of Glass" that we saw before the Throne in chapter 4: 6. Then it was unoccupied, now it is occupied. Then its surface was crystal clear and plain, now its surface is of a "**fiery**" aspect, symbolizing the "**fiery trials**" of its occupants. The occcupants of this "Sea of Glass" come out of the Great Tribulation, for they have gotten the victory over the "Beast," and over his "**Image**," and over his Mark, and over the "**Number of his Name**" and they have harps, and they sing the "**SONG OF MOSES**" and the "**SONG OF THE LAMB**." They are the "Harpers" of chapter 14: 2, whose song only the 144,000 "Sealed Ones" could sing. John only heard them then, now he sees them. That they could sing both the "Song of Moses" and the "Song of the Lamb" implies that they were all or in part Israelites. Some think that the "Song of Moses" that they sung was the song the Children of Israel sang on the shore of the Red Sea after their escape from Egypt, as said in Ex. 15: 1-22, while others think it is Moses' "SWAN SONG" as read in Deu. 31: 19, 22; 31: 30; 32: 43. They sang the "Song of the Lamb" because as Israelites they had been redeemed by the blood of the Lamb.

THE TABERNACLE OF TESTIMONY (REV. 15: 5-8).

John now looks and behold, the Temple of the '**TABERNACLE OF TESTIMONY**' in Heaven was opened: and the 'Seven Angels' came out of the Temple, having the '**SEVEN PLAGUES**,' The "Seven Angels" that comes out of it are clothed in priestly garments, and the "Golden Vials" that they carry were given them by one of the "Beasts" or Living Creatures, and when he gave them to them, the Heavenly Temple was filled with **smoke**. The fact that there were **smoke** takes us back to the Tabernacle that was finished by Moses, and the Temple by Solomon, thiers had a "**cloud**," representing the "Shekinah Glory," but no **smoke**. (Ex. 40: 34-36). (I King 8: 10-11). The "cloud" means **GRACE**, the "**smoke**" means **JUDGMENT**. (Isa. 6: 1-4, Ex. 19: 18).

FIRST VIAL. (BOILS—REV. 16: 1-2).

These "Vial Judgments" are yet **future**, and will be literally fulfilled, and this will give us the "**KEY**" to the **LITERALNESS** of the whole book of Revelation. That these "Vial Judgments" are not figurative is clear from the fact that 4 of the 7 have actually happened before. They are simply repetitions of the "**PLAGUES OF EGYPT**." This Plague of a "**NOISOME AND GRIEVOUS SORE**" that shall fall upon men, is a repetition of the "plague of Boils" that fell upon the Egyptians at the time of the Exodus. (Ex. 9: 8-12). The "First Vial Judgment" then will be a repetition of the "Sixth Egyptian Plague." That, that Plague actually happened, no believer of the Bible doubts, then there is no reason we should try to explain away the literalness of the Plagues that shall follow the pouring out of each of these Vials.

Boils are caused by bad blood, and reveal corruption in the system. These "**grievous sores**" which will come upon MEN ONLY, and not upon the beasts also as in the time of Moses, will not only reveal corruption in the body, but in the heart of those whose sins will cause corruption in their bodies. That these "**sores**" are reserved for those who have the "**MARK OF THE BEAST**," and who worship his **IMAGE** is further proof that these "Vial Judgments" are still **future**. Here is the fulfillment of Rev. 14: 9-11.

The effect of the Plague of Boils upon the Egyptians was to harden their hearts, and a like effect will be produced upon the followers of Antichrist by the Plagues that shall follow the pouring out of the "**Vials**," for we read in verse 9, of chapter 16, that men will blaspheme God, and refuse to repent. From this we see that suffering alone does not lead to repentance.

SECOND VIAL. (BLOOD ON THE SEA.---REV. 16: 3).

We saw that at the sounding of the "Second Trumpet," that the third part of the sea became blood, and the third part of the creatures which were in the sea, and had life, died; and the third part of the ships were destroyed. (Rev. 8: 8-9). But here the whole of the sea is affected. This may mean only the Sea of Galilee, or the Mediterranean Sea, and not the oceans of the earth. It does not follow that this blood is that of men. It may be only of the living creatures that are in the sea. The blood is certainly not the blood of sailors and marines caused by some great naval battle. The inference is that the creatures in the sea died, not because of the loss of their own blood, but because the waters of the sea became "AS the blood of a dead man"-- that is, corrupt.

THIRD VIAL. (BLOOD ON THE RIVERS.---REV. 16: 4-7).

This is a repetition of the "First Egyptian Plague." (Ex. 7: 19-24). When the waters of Egypt were turned into blood all the fish died, but here nothing is said about the inhabitants of the rivers and ponds. Then John heard the "**Angel of the waters**" say---"Thou art righteous, O Lord, which art, and wast, and shall be, because Thou hast judged thus. For they have **shed the blood of saints and prophets**, and Thou hast given them **BLOOD TO DRINK**; for they are worthy." Or deserve it. As a confirmation of the saying of the "Angel of the Waters," reveals the fact that even certain divisions of nature are controlled by angels.

FOURTH VIAL. (GREAT HEAT.---REV. 16: 8-9).

Under the "Fourth Trumpet" the **third part** of the Sun was smitten, and the third part of the Moon and of the Stars; so as the third part of them was darkened, and the day shone not for a third part of it, and the night likewise. (Rev. 8: 12). But it was only the light that was diminished, nothing is said about the heat of the Sun. This "Fourth Vial" is therefore not a recurrence of the "Fourth Trumpet." Here the heat of the Sun is intensified, and so great is the heat that men are scorched by it. This is the time spoken of by Malachi. "Behold, the day cometh that shall **BURN AS AN OVEN**; AND ALL THE PROUD, yea, and all that do wickedly, shall be stubble; and the day that cometh shall burn them up, saith the Lord of Hosts; that it shall leave them neither root nor branch"; and the time is located as just before the "**SUN OF RIGHTEOUSNESS**" shall arise with healing in His wings. (Mal. 4: 1-2). The effect of this Plague will be not to make men repent, but to cause them to **blaspheme the name of God**. Blessed will those people be who do not live to see that day.

FIFTH VIAL. (DARKNESS---REV. 16: 10-11).

This is a repetition of the "Ninth Egyptian Plague," that of **DARKNESS**. (Ex. 10: 21-23). This is the "day" spoken of by Joel. "A day of **darkness** and of **gloominess**, a day of **clouds** and of **thick darkness**. (Joel 2: 1-2). Christ speaks of it in Mark 13: 24, as the time when "the Sun shall be darkened, and the Moon shall not give her light."

This plague shall immediately follows the Plague of "Scorching Heat," as if God in mercy would hide the Sun whose rays had been so hard to bear. The effect of the darkness was to make men gnaw their tongues for PAIN and for their SORES, showing that these plagues overlapped each other, or followed in such rapid order that they were not over the sufferings of one before they were suffering from another, and that they were limited to a short period of a few months, and not distributed over a period of years as they are claimed by the Historical school of interpretation. Their sufferings brought no repentance, but caused them to blaspheme the God of Heaven. This Plague extends over the whole Kingdom of the Beast.

SIXTH VIAL. (THE EUPHRATES DRIED UP.---REV. 16: 12).

This is the literal river Euphrates. The other Plagues will be real, then this will endeed be the drying up of the real Euphrates River. The opening up of a dry passage through the Red Sea that the Children of Israel might escape from Egypt, and the parting of the waters of the River Jordan that they might pass over into the land of canaan, are facts of history, why then shall not the river Euphrates be dried up that the Kings of the East and their armies may cross over and assemble for the Battle of Armageddon? This time is spoken of in Isa. 11: 15-16, "the Lord shall utterly destroy the tongue of the Egyptian Sea (Red Sea), and. . . . shake His hand over the River (Euphrates) and smite its seven streams, so men can go over '**DRY SHOD**'," The Kings shall journey East from Africa, and West from Asia that they may meet in Palestine for the "Battle of Armageddon." The drying up of the Euphrates will serve a twofold purpose. It will permit the remnant of Israel from Assyria to return, and also allow the nations of the far East to be gathered for the "Judgment of Nations." (Matt. 25: 31-46).

THE INTERVAL BETWEEN THE "SIXTH" AND "SEVENTH" VIALS.

THREE UNCLEAN SPIRITS. (Rev. 16: 13-16).

John now tells us how the "Kings of the Earth" and their armies are to be gathered for the "Battle of Armageddon." "**THREE UNCLEAN SPIRITS**" like frogs, will come one out of the mouth of the "Dragon," one out of the mouth of the "Beast," and one out of the mouth of the "False Prophet." John did not say that they were frogs, just that they were <u>like</u> frogs. That they are not real frogs is clear from their miracle working power. They are the "**SPIRITS OF DEMONS**," working miracles, which go forth unto the "Kings of the Earth," and of the whole world, to gather them to the "Battle of that Great Day of God almighty." They are the "Seducing Spirits" who go forth preaching the "**DOCTRINE OF DEVILS**" in the "latter times" of whom Paul warns Timothy. (I Tim. 4: 1). They are sent out by the "**SATANIC TRINITY**," (the dragon; the Beast; and the False Prophet,) on a miracle working ministry.

They are "frog-like" in that they come forth out of the pestiferous quagmires of dardness, do their devilish work in the evening shadows of the day, and creep, and croak, and defile, and fill the ears of the nations with their noisy demonstrations, until they set the kings and armies of the nations in enthusiastic commotion and movement toward the Holy Land to crush out the effort to establish the Kingdom of Christ obn earth. There is an illustration of their method and purpose in the story of the destruction of King Ahab. (I Kings 22: 20-38).

The power of a delusive and enthusiastic sentiment, however engendered, to lead to destruction great hosts of men is seen in the Crusades to recover the Holy Sepulchre at Jerusalem. If a religious fanaticism could, at nine different times, cause hundreds of thousands of religious devotees to undergo unspeakable hardships for a religious purpose, what will not the **miracle working wonders** of the "**FROG-LIKE DEMONS**" of the last days of this Dispensation not be able to do in arousing whole nations, and creating vast armies to march in all directions from all countries, headed by their

Kings, for the purpose of preventing the establishment of the Kingdom of the King of Kings in His own Land of Palestine?

SEVENTH VIAL. (GREAT HAIL.----REV. 16: 17-21).

It is worthy of note that at the breaking of the "Seventh **SEAL**," and the sounding of the "Seventh **TRUMPET**," and the pouring out of the "Seventh **VIAL**," that the same things occur. That is, voices and thunderings are heard, great lightning is seen, and there is a **GREAT EARTHQUAKE**. And at the sounding of the "Seventh **TRUMPET**," and the pouring out of the "Seventh **VIAL**" there is a **GREAT HAIL STORM**. This only confirms what has been already stated, that the "**SEVENTH SEAL**" includes the "Trumpets" and "Vials," and that the "SEVENTH TRUMPET" includes the "Vials," and that the "**SEVENTH TRUMPPET**" includes the "Vials," and that what happens during the "Seventh **SEAL**," and the "Seventh **TRUMPET**," and the "Seventh **VIAL**," all refers to the same period, the "**END OF THE WEEK**." In other words, the opening of the "Seventh **SEAL**" reveals the events that are about to happe, n; the blast of the "Seventh **TRUMPET**" announces the events as forth-comiudesng, and the outpouring of the "Seventh **VIAL**" executes them.

When the "Sevtitenth **SEAL**" was broken there were "**SILENCE**" IN Heaven, but when the "Seventh TRUMPET" sounded, and the "Seventh **VIAL**" was poured out there were "**GREAT VOICES**" in Heaven. These "**Great Voices**" was from the Throne, and they cried—"**IT IS DONE**." When Christ gave up His life on the cross He cried—"**IT IS FINISHED**," which ment, the way and plan of Salvation was complete, and this voice from the throne that cries "**IT IS DONE**" may very well be His voice, announcing that the pouring out of the "Seventh Vial" finishes the wrath of God.

The "Great Earthquake" that follows will be the greatest that this world has ever seen. It is spoken of in Zech. 14: 4-7. So great will it be, that it will level the mountains, and destroy islands, and so change the contour and shape of the

Land of Palestine and the surrounding countries and seas, as to make new maps of that part of the world necessary; and it will raise the Dead Sea so that its waters shall flow again into the Red Sea. (Ez. 47: 1-12). It will divide the "Great City" Jerusalem into 3 parts, and the cities of the nations (the "Ten Federated Nations"), and "**GREAT BABYLON,**" will be destroyed in that "Great Earthquake." This reference to the "City of Babylon" is incidental proof that the City of Babylon at some time, is to be rebuilt. Among the cities destroyed in that Earthquake will be Rome, Naples, London, Paris, and Constantinople.

At that time there will fall upon men a "GREAT HAIL." Each stone will weigh about 100 pounds (a Talent). This appears to be a repetition of the "**SEVENTH EGYPTIAN PLAGUE.**" (Ex. 9: 13-35). Hail has been one of God's methods of destruction. He used it to discomfit the enemies of Israel at Beth-horon in the days of Joshus. (Josh. 10: 11). Their "Law" required that the "Blasphemer" should be "**STONED TO DEATH**" (Lev. 24: 16), and these Blasphemers of the "End Time" shall be **STONE FROM HEAVEN**.

The "Seventh Vial" covers the "**WHOLE PERIOD**" from the time the "Seventh Angel" pours out its contents until Christ returns to the Mount of Olives. For the earthquake that splits the Mount of Olives, upheaves the land of Palestine, levels mountains, submerges islands, and destroys the cities of the Nations, along with the City of Babylon, is cause by the touch of Christ's feet on the Mount of Olives at the Revelation stage of His Second Coming (Zech. 14: 4), and the "Great Hail" in all probability will not fall until the time comes in the crisis of the Battle of Amageddon for the destruction of the allied armies of Antichrist. Hailstones will be the missiles used by the Armies of Heaven.

In Rev. 19:15, we are told that out of the mouth of Christ, at His return, will go a "**SHARP SWORD,**" that with it He should smite the nations, and in II Thess. 2: 8, we are told that Antichrist (The wicked one), shall be consumed by the

"**SPIRIT OF THE LORD'S MOUTH.**" Whether we take these statement as literal or not, it is clear that they stand for some **supernatural means of destruction**, and refer more to the followers of Antichrist, than to Antichrist himself, for he personally is not to be destroyed, but is to be cast **ALIVE** into the "Lake of Fire." (Rev. 19: 20).

As the pouring out of the "Seventh Vial" finishes the "Wrath of God," it is in harmony with the purposes of the Book of Revelation to foretell at this point what will then happen to the enemies of God still present. These we will now examine under the heading of the "Seven Doom."

THE SEVEN DOOMS.

FIRST DOOM. ECCCLESIASTICAL BABYLON.

"MYSTERY BABYLON THE GREAT." (Rev. 17: 1-18).

It is clear, That the ancient city of Babylon restored is to play an important part in the startling events of the last days of this Dispensation. We see this from what is said of it in the seventeenth and eighteenth chapters of the book of Revelation. At first sight the two chapters, which contain some things in common, are difficult to understand, but when we get the "**Key**" the understanding becomes easy.

The seventeenth chapter speaks of a "**Woman,**" and this "Woman" is called

**"MYSTERY,
BABYLON THE GREAT,
THE MOTHER OF HARLOTS AND
ABOMINATIONS OF THE EARTH."**

The eighteenth chapter speaks of a "City," a literal city, called "Babylon the Great." That the "Woman" and the "City does not represent the same thing is clear, for what is said of the "woman" does not apply to a city, and what is said of the "City" does not apply to a woman. The "**Woman**" is destroyed by the "**Ten Kings,**" while the "**Kings of the Earth**" in the next chapter, "**bewail and lament**" the destruction of the "City," which is not destroyed by them, but by a mighty earthquake and fire. Again the "**Woman**" is destroyed **three and a half years BEFORE THE CITY**; and the fact that the first verse of chapter eighteen says ---"**after these things,**" that is after the destruction of the "Woman," what happen to the "City" occurs, shows that the "Woman" and the "City" are not one and the same.

The "Woman's name is---"**MYSTERY, Babylon the Great.**" The word "Mystery" refers to something not fully understood or understandable; a mysterious quality. Paul calls the Church a "Mystery" because it was not known to the Old Testament Patriarchs and Prophets. (Eph. 3: 1-21). That Christ was to have a "Bride" was first revealed to Paul in (Eph. 5: 23-32), and the "Mystery" that Antichrist is to have a "bride" was frist revealed to John on the Isle of Patmos. And guest what? The name of Antichrist's "bride" is also "Babylon the Great." Someone may ask why give to a "bride" the name of a "City"? The answer is that it is not so unusual in the Scriptures. When the same angel that showed John in this chapter "Mystery, Babylon the Great," came to him in chapter 21: 9-10 and said---"Come hither, I will show thee the Bride---"**The Lamb's Wife**'," he showed John, instead of a woman, that great City, the "Holy Jerusalem" descending out of Heaven from God. We see here that a "city" is called a "bride" because of its inhabitants, and not the city itself, are the **bride.** "Mystery, Babylon the Great," the "Bride" of Antichrist, then, is not a literal city, but a "System," a religious and apostate "System." As the Church, the Bride of Christ, is composed of regenerated followers of Christ, so "Mystery, Babylon the Great," the bride of Antichrist, will be composed of the followers of all **False Religions**.

The river Euphrates, on which the City of Babylon was built, was one of the four branches into which the river that flowed through the Garden of Eden was divided, and Satan probably chose the site of Babylon as his headquarters from which to sally forth to tempt Adam and Eve. It was proberly here that the antediluvian Apostasy had its source that ended in the Flood. To this centre the "forces of Evil" gravitated after the flood, and "**Babel**" was the result. This was the origin of nations, but the nations were not scattered abroad over the earth until Satan had implanted in them the "Virus" of a doctrine that has been the source of every false religion the world has ever known.

Babel, or Babylon, was built by Nimrod. (Gen. 10: 8-10). It was the seat of the first great Apostasy. Here the "**Babylonian Cult**" was invented. A system claiming to possess the highest wisdom and to reveal the divinest secrets. Before a member could be initated he had to "confess" to the Priest. The Priest then had him in his power. This is the secret of the power of the Priests of the Roman Catholic Church today. Once admitted into this order, men were no longer Babylonians, Assyrians, or Egyptians, but members of a **Mystical Brotherhood**, over whom was placed a Pontiff or "High Priest," whose word was law. The city of Babylon conyinued to be the seat of Satan until the fall of the Babylonian and Medo-Persian Empires, when he shifted his Capital to Pergamos inAsia Minor, where it in John's day. (Rev. 2: 12, 13).

When Attalus, the Pontiff and King of Pergamos, died in B. C. 133, he bequeathed the Headship of the "Babylonian Priesthood" to Rome. When the Etruscans came to Italy from Lydia (the region of Pergamos), they brought with them the Babylonian religion and rites. They set up a Pontiff who was head of the Priesthood. Soon after the Romans accepted this Pontiff as their civil ruler. Julius Caesar was made Pontiff of the Etruscan Order in B. C. 74. In B. C. 63 he became "Supreme Pontiff" of the "Babylonian Order," Thus becoming heir to the rights and titles of Attalus, Pontiff of Pergamos, who had made Rome his heir by will. Making the first Roman Emperor the head of the "Babylonian Priesthood," and Rome the successor of Babylon. The Emperors of Rome continued to exercise the office of "Supreme Pontiff" until A. D. 376, when the Emperor Gratian, for Christian reasons, refused it. The Bishop of the Church at Rome, Damasus, was elected to the position. He had been Bishop 12 years, having been made Bishop in A. D. 366, through the influence of the monks of Mt. Carmel, a college of Babylonian religion originally founded by the priests of Jezebel. So in A. D. 378 the Head of the "Babylonian Order" became the ruler of the "Roman Church." Thus Satan united **Rome and Babylon Into One Religious System**.

Soon after Damasus was made "supreme Pontiff" the "rites" of Babylon began to come to the front. The worship of the virgin Mary was set up in A. D. 381. At that time, All the outstanding festivals of the Roman Catholic Church were of Babylonian origin. Easter is not a Christian name, it means "Ishtar," one of the titles of the Babylonian (supposably) Queen of Heaven, whose worship by the Children of Israel was such an abomination in the sight of God. The decree for the observance of Easter and Lent was given in A. D. 519. The "Rosary" is of Pagan origin. There is **nothing** writting in the word of God for the use of the "Sign of the Cross." Its origins came in the mystic "**TAU**" of the Chaldeans and Egyptians. It came from the letter "**T**" the initial name of "**Tammuz**," and was used in the "Babylonian Mysteries" for the same magic purposes as the Romish Church of today employs it. Celibacy, the Tonsure, and the Order of Monks and Nuns, have no warrant or authority from Bible Scripture. The Nuns are mere imitations of the "**Vestal Virgins**" of Pagan Rome.

When we look at the word "**Mystery**," the Papal Church has always shrouded herself in mystery. The mystery of "Baptismal Regeneration"; the mystery of "Miracle and Magic" whereby the simple memorials of the Lord's Supper are changed by the mysterious word "Transubstantiation," from simple bread and wine into the **literal Body and Blood of Christ**; the mystery of the "**Holy Water**"; the mystery of "**Lights on the Altar**," the "**Mystery Plays,**" and other superstitious rites and ceremonies mumbled in a language that tends to mystery, and tends to confusion which is the meaning of the word Babylon.

All this was a "Mystery" in John's day, because the "Papal Church" had not as yet developed; though the "Mystery of Iniquity" was already at work (II. Thess. 2: 7), but it is no longer a "Mystery" for it is now easy to identify the "Woman"---"Mystery, Babylon the Great," which John described, as the "**Papal Church**."

In Rev. 17: 4 we read that the "Woman" "was arrayed in purple and scarlet color, and decked with gold and precious stones and pearls, having a '**Golden Cup**' in her hand full of **abominations and filthiness of her fornications**".

Now who does not know that scarlet and purple are the colors of the Papacy? Of the different articles of attire specified for the Pope to wear when he is installed into office, five are **scarlet**. A vest covered with pearls, and a mitre, adorned with gold and precious stones was also to be worn. How completely this answers the description of the Woman's dress as she sits upon the Scarlet Colored Beast. Mul

We are also told that the Woman was "drunken with the blood of the Saints, and with the **blood of the Martyrs of Jesus**." While this refers more particularly to the martyrs of the time of Antichrist, yet who does not know, who has studied the history of the Christian Church for the past nineteen centuries, that this is true of the Papal Church during those centuries?

The fact that the Woman sits on a "Scarlet Colored Beast" reveals the fact that at that time the Beast (Antichrist) will support the Woman in her ecclesiastical pretension, or in other words, the Woman, as a "State Church," will control and rule the State, and her long dream of world-wide Ecclesiastical Supremacy will at last be realized, for John tells us that "the waters which thou sawest, where the '**whore**' **sitteth**, are **Peoples**, and **Multitudes**, and **Nations** and **Tongues**." That means that after the "True Church" (the Bride of Christ) is taken out of the world the "**False**" or "**Papal Church**" (the bride of Antichrist) will remain, and the professing body of Christians (having the "form of Godliness without the power") left behind. Will largely enter the Papal Church, and it will become the **Universal Church**. But this will continue for only a short time, for the "Ten Kings" of the "Federated Kingdom," finding their power curtailed by the "Papal System" will "**hate**

the Whore," and strip her of her gorgeous apparel, confiscate her wealth (eat her flesh) and burn her churches and cathedrals with fire. (Rev. 17: 16). This will occur at the time the worship of the Beast is set up, for Antichrist in his jealous hate will not permit any worship that does not centre in himself.

The Beast upon which the Woman sits is introduced to show from whom the Woman (the Papal Church) gets her power and support after the True Church has been "caught out," and also to show that the Beast (Antichrist) and the Woman (the Papal Church) are not one and the same, but separate. Therefore the Papacy can not be Antichrist. From this foreview of the Papacy we see that the Papal Church is not a dying "System." That she is to be revived and become a "**Universal Church,**" and in doing so, she is to commit fornication with the Kings of the earth, and that she shall again be "drunk with the blood" of the martyrs of the Tribulation Period. The meaning of chapter seventeen of the book of RevelaPtion is no Mystery; The prophetic portrait of the Woman given there, corresponds too closely with the history of the Papal Church to be a mere coincidence.

SECOND DOOM. COMMERCIAL BABYLON. (REV. 18: 1-24).

This chapter begins with the words "**after these things**." What things? The things recorded in the previous chapter, the **destruction** of "**Mystical Babylon.**"

If "**Mystical Babylon.**" Was destroyed in chapter seventeen, then she cannot appear in this chapter, and as thus, the City here described must be a literal city called Babylon, and as there is no city of that name on the earth today, that I am aware of, nor has there been since the ancient city of Babylon was destroyed, it must refer to some future city named Babylon. That the two chapters refer to different things is further verified by the fact that they are announced by different angels. The events of Chapter seventeen are announced by one of the "Vial" Angels, while those of chapter eighteen are announced by "another" angel; probably the "Second Angel Messenger," who by way of anticipation, announced in chapter 14: 8, the "Fall of Babylon," that was called---"**That Great City.**"

The ancient city of Babylon from the days of Nimrod (Gen. 10: 10), grew in size and importance century after century until it reached its greatest glory in the reign of Nebuchadnezzar B. C. 604-562. As described by Herodotus it was an exact square of 15 miles on a side, or 60 miles around, and surrounded by a brick wall 87 feet thick, and 350 feet high (listed), though probably that is a mistake, 100 feet being nearer the height. On the wall were 250 towers, and the top of the wall was wide enough to allow 6 chariots to drive abreast. Outside this wall was a vast ditch surrounding the city, kept filled with water from the river Euphrates; and inside the wall, and not far from it, was another wall, not much inferior, but narrower, extending around the city.

There were twenty-five avenues, 150 feet wide, that ran across the city from North to South, and the same number crossed them at right angles from east to west, and the city was divided into two equal parts by the river Euphrates, that flowed diagonally through it, and whose banks, within the city, were walled up, and pierced with brazen gates, with steps leading down to the river. At the ends of the main avenues and on each side of the city were gates, whose leaves were of brass, that shone as they were opened or closed in the rising or setting of the sun, like "leaves of flame."

That part of the Euphrates that was within the city, was spanned by a bridge, and at each end was a beautiful palace, and these palaces were connected by a subterranean passageway, underneath the bed of the river, in which at different points were located beautiful banqueting rooms constructed entirely of brass.

Near one of these palaces stood the "Tower of Babel," consisting of 8 towers, each 75 feet high, rising one upon the other, with an outside winding stairway to its summit, which towers, with the Chapel on the top, made a height of 660 feet. This Chapel contained the most expensive furniture of any place of worship in the world. One golden image alone, 45 feet high, was valued at $17,500,000.00, (Seventeen Million, five hundread thousand dollars) and the whole of the sacred utensils were reckoned to be worth $200, 000,000.00.

Babylon also contained one of the "Seven Wonders" of the world, the famous **Hanging Gardens**. These Gardens were 400 feet square, and were raised in terraces one above the other to the height of350 feet, and were reached by stairways 10 feet wide. The top of each terrace was covered with large stones, on which was laid a bed of rushes, then a thick layer of asphalt, then two courses of brick, cemented together, and finally plates of lead to prevent leakage; the whole was then covered with dirt and planted with shrubbery and large trees. The whole Gardens had the appearance from a distance, of a forest-covered mountain, which would be a remarkable sight in the level plain of the Euphrates. These Gardens were built by Nebuchadnezzar simply to please his wife, who came from the mountainous country of Media, and who was, then made contented with her surroundings. The character of its inhabitants and of its official life is seen in the description of "Belshazzar's Feast." (Dan. 5: 1-31).

Babylon was probably the most magnificent city the world had ever seen, and its fall reveals what a city may become when it forsakes God and He sends His judgment upon it. Babylon was so intimately connected with the history of God's people that the scriptures have much to say about it. A large part of the book of Daniel and of the prophecy of Jeremiah relate to it, and it is mentioned in 11 other books of the Old Testament, and in 4 of the New Testament. And that the Book of Revelation is a continuation of the Book of Daniel is further proven by the fact that the city of Babylon is again spoken of in it, and its prominence in the affairs of the world at the "End Time" is disclosed, and its final destruction is foretold.

THE CITY OF BABYLON TO BE REBUILT.

Since all the Old Testament prophecies in reference to the ancient city of Babylon's destruction have been literally fulfilled; How can we affirm that it is to be rebuilt and destroyed all over again?

As there is no city with equal quality as the ancient city of Babylon in existence today, The references in the Book of Revelation to the destruction of such a city must be symbolical and not referring to a literal city.

By turning to Isaiah, chapter 13 and 14, and Jeremiiah, chapter 50 and 51, we find a description of Babylon and her destruction. In these two prophecies we find much that has not as yet been fulfilled in regard to the city of Babylon. Now the city of Babylon was captured in B. C. 541 by Cyrus, who was mentioned "by name" in prophecy 125 years before he was born, in B. C. 712. (Isa. 44: 28; 45: 4). So quietly and quickly was the city taken on the night of Belshazzar's Feast by draining the river that flowed through the city, and entering by the river bed, and the gates that surmounted its banks, that the Babylonian guards had forgotten to lock that night, however, some of the inhabitants did not know until the "third" day that the King had been killed and the city taken. The city was not destroyed at that time. Some years after it revolted against Darius Hystaspis, and after a fruitless siege of nearly 20 months the city of Babylon was taken by strategy. This was in B. C. 516.

In B. C. 331 Alexander the Great approached the city which was then so powerful and flourishing that he made preparation for bringing all his forces into action in case it should offer resistance, but the citizens threw open the gates and received him with acclamations. After sacrificing to "Bel," or Babel, Alexander the Great let it be known that he would rebuild the vast temple of that god, and for weeks he kept 10,000 men employed in clearing away the ruins from the foundations, intending to revive the glory of Babylon and make it his capital, when his purpose was defeated by his sudden death of marsh-fever and intemperance in his thirty-third year.

During the subsequent wars of his generals Babylon suffered much and finally came under the power of Seleucus, who, prompted by ambition to build a Capital for himself, founded Seleucia in its neighborhood about B. C. This rival city gradually drew off the inhabitants of Babylon, so that Strabo, who died in A. D. 25, speaks of the latter as being to a great extent deserted. Nevertheless the Jews left from the Captivity still resided there in large numbers, and in A. D. 60 we find the Apostle Peter working among them, for it was from Babylon that Peter wrote his Epistle (I Peter 5: 13), addressed "to the strangers scattered throughout Pontus, Galatia, Cappadocia, Asia and Bithynia."

About the middle of the 5th century Theodoret speaks of Babylon as being inhabited only by Jews, who had still three Jewish Universities, and in the last year of the same century the "Babylonian Talmud" was issued, and recognized as authoritative by the Jews of the whole world.

In about A. D. 1100 Babylon seems to have once again grown into a town of some importance, for it was then known as the "Two Mosques." Shortly afterwards it was enlarged and fortified and received the name of Hillah, or "Rest." In A. D. 1898 Hillah contained about 10,000 inhabitants, and was surrounded by fertile lands, and abundant date groves stretched along the banks of the Euohrates. Certainly it has never been true that "neither shall the Arabian pitch tents there, neither shall the shepherds make their fold there." (Isa. 13: 20). Nor can it be said of Babylon---"Her cities are a desolation, a dry land, and a wilderness, a land wherein no man dwelleth, neither doth any son of man pass thereby." (Jer. 51: 43). Now Hillah was entirely constructed from the debris, and even in the houses of Bagdad, Babylonian stamped bricks may be frequently noticed.

However, in the book of Isaiah it is more specific, for he locates the **Time** when his prophecy will be fulfilled. He calls it the **"Day of the Lord."** (Isa. 13: 9). And he locates it at the beginning of the millennium, or during the events that usher in the Millennium, for he says---**"The stars of heaven and the constellations thereof shall not give their light; the sun shall be darkened in his going forth, and the moon shall not cause her light to shine."** (Isa. 13: 10); (Luke 21: 25-27).

Surely nothing like this happened when Babylon was taken by Cyrus.

In the description of the destruction of the city of Babylon given in Rev. 18, we read that her judgment will come in **one hour** (Rev 18: 10), and that in one hour she shall be made desolate (vs.19), and as an illustration of the suddenness and completeness of her destruction, a mighty angel took up a stone like a great Millstone, and cast it into the sea, saying--- "Thus with Violence shall that great city Babylon be thrown down and shall be found no more at all." (Rev. 18: 21). We are also told in the same chapter that she is to be destroyed by **FIRE**(Rev. 18: 8, 9, 18), and this is in exact harmony with the words of Isa. 13: 19. "And Babylon, the glory of Kingdoms, the beauty of the Chaldees' excellency, shall be as when God overthrew **Sodom and Gomorrah**;" and the Prophet Jeremiah mades the same statement in Jeremiah 50: 40.

The detruction of Sodom and Gomorrah was not protracted through many centuries, their glory disappeared in a few hours (Gen. 19: 24-28), and as ancient Babylon was not destroyed then, the prophecies of Isaiah and Jeremiah cannot be fulfilled unless there is to be a future Babylon that shall also be destroyed.

In Rev. 16: 17-19, we are told that Babylon shall be destroyed by an earthquake, attended with most vivid and continuous lightning and awful thunder. It would appear then, that as Sodom and Gomorrah were first set on fire and then swallowed up by an earthquake, that the rebuilt city of Babylon will be set on fire, and as the site of ancientBabylon is underlaid with asphalt, that an earthquake will break up the crust of the earth, and hurl down the burning city into a

"**Lake of Fire**," and the city like a "**Millstone**" (Rev. 18: 21) will sink below the surface of the earth as into the sea, and be swallowed up so that it will be impossible to ever take of her stones for building purposes, and the land shall become a wilderness where no man shall ever dwell.

The fact that in her will be found the blood of the Prophets, and Holy Apostles and Saints (Rev. 18: 20, 24), shows that the Papal Church is not in view in this eighteenth chapter, for there was no Papal Church in Old Testament times, or in the days of the Apostles. It is the ancient as well as the revived **City of Babylon** that is meant. For in Old Testament days the blood of the Prophets was shed by the "Babylonish System" of false religions as visualized in the City of Babylon. So that it can truthfully be said that the blood of Prophets and Apostles of all ages has been shed by her.

THE EPHAH OF COMMERCE.

There is a remarkable prophetic vision recorded by the Prophet Zechariah in Zech. 5: 5-11. The "EPHAH" which Zechariah saw go forth, was the largest of Hebrew dry measures, and is often used as a symbol of Commerce, and its "resemblance," or going forth through all the earth, that probably refers to **UNIVERSAL COMMERCIALISM**. In this "Ephah" sat a "**WOMAN**" who was called "**WICKEDNESS**." This "**WOMAN**" attempted to rise but the Angel thrust her back, and replaced the lid made of a "**Talent of Lead**." Then "**Two Women**," with the wings of a Stork, came, and lifted the "Ephah" high in the air and carried it with the swiftness of the wind to the "**LAND OF SHINAR**" to build her a **HOUSE**. Now the "**LAND OF SHINAR**" was the place where they built the Tower of Babel (Gen. 11: 1-9), on whose site ancient **BABYLON** was located. Since this vision of the Prophet occurred many years after the fall of ancient Babylon, the HOUSE that is to be built for this "Ephah," or the "**WOMAN**" who was transported in it, must be built in some future City of Babylon.

As we have seen the "Ephah" stands for **COMMERCE**, and as the occupant of the "Ephah" is called "**WICKEDNESS**," it reveals the fact that the "Commercialism" of the time of the vision's fulfilment will be characterized by all manner of dishonest schemes and methods. And the fact that the "WOMAN" is thrust back into the "Ephah" and covered with a "Talent of Lead," indicates that those dishonest schemes and methods are to be kept out of sight.

This vision of the "Ephah" by the Prophet Zachariah is more confirmatory proof that the ancient City of Babylon is to be rebuilt and become the **COMMERCIAL CENTRE OF THE WORLD**. Every influence political and commercial will favor this, and as the "Stork Winged Woman" will be favored by the "**wings of the wind**," the tendency of Commerialism to that part of the world, when the time comes to carry the "Ephah" to the "Land of Shinar," we can see that it will not take long, with the wealth of the world at the command of the Capitalists of that day, to rebuild Babylon and make it the great Commercial Centre of the world. Once commerce is firmly established in Babylon, the occupant of the "Ephah"---"WICKEDNESS," will lift the lid and reveal herself, and no one will be able to buy or sell but those who has the "**MARK OF THE BEAST**."

As to the probability of the ancient city of Babylon being rebuilt, we have only to consider the events that in years pass have been happening in that part of the world. It can be seen in the department of war in Paris France, records of valuable surveys and maps made by order of Napoleon I, in Babylon, and among them is a plan for a **New City of Babylon**, showing that the vast schemes of Napoleon avocated the **Rebuilding of the Ancient City of Babylon**, and making it his capital, as his ambition was to conquer the whole of Europe and Asia, and he recognized to that end the strategical position of ancient Babylon as a governmental and commercial centre.

It is a fact that the whole countries of Mesopotamia, Assyria and Babylonia, only needs a system of irrigation to make it again the most fertile country in the world, with steps having already been taken in that direction. In 1850 the British Government sent out a military officer with his command to survey and explore the river Euphrates at a cost of $150,000, and when the Euphratean valley for the purpose of constructing a series of irrigation canals that would restore the country and make it again the great grain producing country it once was. As a result towns and cities would spring up and railroads would be built.

With these facts in mind it can readily be seen that it is the purpose of European capitalists to revive the country of Babylonia and rebuild its cities, and when the time comes the city of Babylon will be rebuilt almost in a night and on a scale of magnificence, such as the world has never seen. The rapid growth of modern cities is one of the remarkable phenomena of the times.

Since 1880 more than 600 cities have been built in America. A little more than 100 years ago the site of the City of Chicago was but a swampy expanse at the mouth of the Chicago river. Now it has been transformed into a beautiful Metropolis, stretching 25 miles along the shore of Lake Michigan, with more than 5000 miles of streets, many of them beautiful boulevards 120 feet wide, called Highways. In 1840 Chicago had only 4470 inhabitants, today the population is over 4,000,000. Once the Capitalists of the world are ready, the revived City of Babylon will spring up in a few years.

It has been said by some that we can expect Jesus to return at "**any moment**," However, shouldn't the City of Babylon be rebuilt before He can return? There is not a word in Scripture that says that Jesus cannot come and take away His Church until Babylon is rebuilt. At this time period (2016), the Church may be taken out of the world years before that happens, at Jesus bequest.

Babylon the great will be an immense city, the greatest in every respect the world has ever seen. It will be a typical city, the London's, the Paris's, the Berlin's, the New York's, the Chicago's, the Rome's of it's day. It will be the greatest commercial city of the world. The manufactories will turn out the richest of fabries, and all that genius can invent for the comfort and convenience of men will be found on the market. It will be a city given over to pleasure and business. Business men and promoters will give their days and nights to scheming how to make money fast, and the pleasure loving will be constantly planning new pleasures. There will be riotous joy and ceaseless feasting. As it was in the days of Noah and of lot, they will be marrying and giving in marriage, buying and selling, building and planting.

The blood will run hot in their veins. Money will be their god, pleasure their high-priest, and unbridled passion the ritual of their worship. It will be a city of music. The world's best singers and players will be there. Its theatres and places of music will be going day and night. Its stores and places of business will never close, night or day, or Sunday, for the mad whirl of pleasure and the absorbing desire for riches will keep the wheels of business constantly moving and all this will be easy because the "God of this World"---Satan, will possess the minds and bodies of men and women, for we read in (Rev. 18: 2), that Babylon at that time will be "the **Habitation of Devils**, and the **Hold of Every Foul Spirit, and the cage of every Unclean and Hateful Bird**." The city will be the seat of the most imposing "**OCCULTISM**," and mediums, and those desiring to communicate with the other world, will then go to Babylon, as men and women now go to New York and Paris for fashions and sensuous pleasures. In that day demons, disembodied souls, and unclean spirits will find at Babylon the opportunity of their lives to materialize themselves in human bodies, and from the atmospheric heavens above, and from the Abyss below they will come in countless legions until Babylon shall be full of demons possessed men and women, and at the height of its glory, and just before its fall, Babylon will be ruled by **SATAN HIMSELF**, incarnated in the "Beast"—**ANTICHRIST**.

But before its destruction God will mercifully deliver His own people, for a voice from heaven will cry---"**Come Out of Her, My People, That Ye be Not Partakers of Her Sins, and that Ye Receive Not of Her Plagues**." As Sodom and Gomorrah could not be destroyed until righteous Lot had escaped, so Babylon cannot be destroyed until all the righteous people in it have fled. The destruction of the will be sudden and without warning. A fearful storm will sweep over the city. The lightning and thunder will be incessant (countinueous). The city will be set on fire and a great earthquake will shake it from the centre to the circumference. The tall office buildings, the "Hanging Gardens" and the great towers will totter and fall, the crust of the earth will crack and open, and the whole city with all of its people will sink like a "**Millstone**" (Rev. 18: 21), into a lake of burning bitumen (substance found in asphalt and used for surfacing roads and waterproofing), and the smoke will ascend as of a burning fiery furnace, and the horror of the scene will be intensified by vast clouds of steam, generated by the waters of the Euphrates pouring into that lake of fiery asphalt, and when night comes on those clouds the steam will reflect the light of the burning city so it can be seen for miles in all directions in that level country. And the Kings of the earth, and the merchants, and the shipmasters, and sailors, and all who have peofited by her merchandise, will stand afar off and cry and wail because of her destruction, but the heavens will rejoice for God will have rewarded her Double according to her words, and **BABYLON WILL BE NO MORE**.

THE INTERVAL BETWEEN THE SECOND AND THIRD DOOMS

1. THE HALLELUJAH CHORUS. (REV. 19: 1-7).

After these things. What **things** do we mean? The destruction of "**MYSTICAL BABYLON**" and the restored **CITY OF BABYLON**. The first "Alleluia" is for the destruction of the "**GREAT WHORE**"---"**Mystical Babylon**." The second "**Alleluia**" is for the destruction of the "**CITY OF BABYLON**" whose **smoke** rose up for ever and ever, which could not be said of "Mystical Babylon" but only of a **CITY**. In chapter 18 verse 20, at the destruction of the "City of Babylon," we read---"Rejoice over her, thou Heaven, and ye Holy Apostles and Prophets; for God have avenged you on her." Listern and you will hear the rejoicing; what the merchants, and shipmasters, and sailors, and traders, weep and wail and mourn over, the---"Fall of Babylon," Heaven rejoices over. This shows us the difference between Heaven and Earth's opinion of these Divine Judgments.

Notice that in Rev. 19: verse 1 we have the first occurrence of the word "**HALLELU-JAH**" in the New Testament. It is a compound Hebrew word "**HALLELU-JAH**" ("Praise-Ye-Jah"). It occurs 24 times in the Old Testament, and 4 times in the New Testament. In the Old Testament the word is always translated---"**Praise ye the Lord**," In the New Testament the Greek word "ALLELUIA" is left untranslated, but in the New Version the word "**HALLELUJAH**" is substituted for "**Alleluia**." Four times the word "Hallelujah" is uttered in chapter 19, not only by a great multitude, but by the "Four Beasts," and by the "Four and Twenty Elders." It is the "**cry of victory**" in which praise is ascribed to God. They also sang "Hallelujah" because the time had come for the "**MARRIAGE OF THE LAMB**."

2. THE MARRIAGE OF THE LAMB (REV. 19: 8-10).

It is marvelous how th Holy Spirit have enshrined in the Scriptures the Bride relation of the Church and her Lord. It is revealed to the spiritual mind in the most unexpected places. It is foreshadowed in the Old Testament in the story of Isaac and Rebekah. Many readers of the Bible have wondered why the "**SONG OF SOLOMON**" was ever included among the books of the Old Testament. Upon the first reading, it appears as only a love song of Solomon for one of the many women that he loved. But a careful study of the Song reveals the fact that it is an inspired song of the love of the Church of Christ during His absence in the Heavenlies. The song describes a maiden of Shulam, a Galilean town some 5 miles south of Mt. Tabor, who was taken from her home to one of Solomon's palaces, probably in the Lebanon district, where Solomon tries to win her love. She had lived with her mother, but her brothers had treated her cruelly and made her the keeper of the vine yards until her skin was so dark that she spoke of herself as **"BLACK BUT COMELY,"** and had not kept the vineyard of her own beauty, and her brothers even went so far as to speak disparagingly of her character. But there was one, a shepherd, who loved and believed in her, and whose love she returned with the most intense passion. At times Solomon visited her and sought to win her away from her beloved, but she would not listen to him. During the day she would talk to herself of her lover and imagine she heard his voice calling, and durning the night she dreamt of him and imagined she was walking the streets of the city hunting for him. At times she bursts out in rapturous praise of her lover's beauty, then calls him in loving tones. At last she escapes and finds her lover and they are seen approaching from the meadows happy in each other's love.

What a beautiful picture we have here of the love of the true Church for her absent Lord. Its as though the Church is held captive in this world and is being constantly solicited by the offers of wealth and splendor to withdraw her love from Immanuel, her Shepherd Lover, who is feeding His flock in Paradise, and give her heart to her Solomonic lovers, and consort with the Kings and governments of the world, as does her sister the Harlot Church. But she cannot give her Heavenly Lover up. At times she is sorely tempted, then she sees Him with the eye of faith, and dreams of Him as spiritually present, and she is ravished by the vision of His beauty. Then suddenly He vanishes, and she is alone again carrying on the conflict with the world that tries to cast its spell upon her, and offers her its glories if she would only forsake her Shepherd Lover. But while the temptation is great her love never wavers, for she sees the time approaching when she shall be caught away from the earth to meet her Shepherd Lover on the plains of Paradise.

The "Marriage of the Lamb" was one of the themes that Jesus loved to dwell on. In the Parable of the "Ten Virgins" He tells how the Virgins went out to meet the Bridegroom, and the unpreparedness of some of them to meet Him. And in the Parable of the "Marriage of the King's Son" (Matt. 22: 1-14), He prophetically refers to it, and gives us a foreview of it, and in the verses now under consideration He describes its consummation, saying---"Let us be glad and rejoice and give honor to Him, for the '**MARRIAGE OF THE LAMB**' is come, and His wife have made herself ready. And to her was granted that she should be arrayed in fine linen, clean and white, for the fine linen represents the righteousness of saints. And He saith unto me, write---"**BLESSED ARE THEY WHICH ARE CALLED UNTO THE MARRIAGE SUPPER OF THE LAMB**."

Notice that it does not say the "**Marriage of the Bride**," but the "**MARRIAGE of the LAMB**." That grand event will be not so much the consummation of the hopes of the Bride, as it will be the consummation of the **PLAN OF GOD FOR HIS SON**, arranged for before the Foundation of the World. (Eph. 1: 4).

The "Marriage of the Lamb" is the consummation of the joy of Christ **AS A MAN**. It would not have been possible if Christ had not been born **IN THE FLESH**. Otherwise it would have been the union of dissimilar natures, for the Bride is of human origin. This is why Jesus took His HUMAN NATURE back with Him to glory, and today we have in Heaven the MAN Christ Jesus. (I Tim. 2: 5).

While the Bride was chosen for Him **before** the Foundation of the world, the "**Espousal**"; (Wedding ceremony) could not take place until after Christ assumed humanity, and so it was not until after Christ's incarnation that the apostle Paul could say---"I am jealous over you with godly jealousy: for I have **ESPOUSED** you to one husband, that I may present you as a **CHASTE VIRGIN** to Christ. (II Cor. 11: 2)." There have been many lone betrothals in which the betrothed have been faithful to their vows until the long wait has ended in a happy marriage, but the longest this world has ever heard of is that of Christ waiting for His Bride the Church. He has been waiting now for over 2000 years, but He will not have to wait much longer. Sometime in the near future, the sleeping Church shall hear the cry---"**BEHOLD THE BRIDEGROOM COMETH, GO YE OUT TO MEET HIM**," and Heaven will resound with the cry---"Let us be glad and rejoice, and give honor to Him, for the **MARRIAGE OF THE LAMB IS COME**." (Rev. 19: 7). Ordinarily the most interest in a wedding clusters around the bride, but the intimation in Scripture is, that the most interest at the "Marriage of the Lamb" will centre around the **BRIDEGROOM**. If there is joy in Heaven in the presence of the angels of God over one sinner that repenteth, and that joy is the joy of the FATHER, how much greater will be the joy of the FATHER when He shall behold the consummation of His plan for His Son inHis Marriage to His Bride the Church. There have been many weddings of international interest where the invited guests and specttators witnessed a spectacle magnificent in its appointments, and rejoiced in a union that bound together even different nations. But the wedding of the Lamb and His Bride will surpass them all, for it shall unite Heaven and Earth in a bond that shall never be broken.

Let's take a look at the "Marriage of the Lamb" in more detail. We will ask and try to answer some of the questions that relates to it. Most Biblical Expositors take it for granted that the subject is so familiar to Bible students that it needs no explanation, and so they do not dwell upon it, but this is not so. These difficulties will appear as we try to answer them.

1. WHO IS THE BRIDEGROOM?

To this question there can be but one answer. The "Bridegroom" is the King's SON of the Parable of the "Marriage of the **King's Son**" (Matt. 22: 1-14), or **JESUS**, spoken of as the **LAMB**. John the Baptist spoke of Him as the "**BRIDEGROOM,**" and John spoke of himself as the "**Friend**" of the Bridegroom who rejoiced to hear His voice.(John 3: 29). Jesus also represented **Himself** as the "Bridegroom," saying---"Can the 'Children of the Bride-chamber' mourn as long as the **Bridegroom is with them**." (Matt. 9: 15). And in the Parable of the "Ten Virgins" Jesus refers to Himself as the "Bridegroom." (Matt. 25: 1-10). Therefore, the Bridegroom is Christ.

2. WHO IS THE BRIDE?

Now this answer brings about a difference of opinion. Some claim that the "Bride," because she is called "**WIFE**" in Rev. 19: 7, is **ISRAEL**, because in the Old Testament God calls Himself the **HUSBAND** of Israel. (Isa. 54: 5). Those who advocate this view claim that "**Wife**" is the earthly name of Israel, and "**Bride**" the Heavenly. Some hold that because Isaac's bride was taken from his own Kin, that, therefore, to complete the type, Jesus' Bride must be Israel, His own Kin, and not the Church composed mainly of Gentiles. But we must not forget that while Abraham was the first Hebrew his Kin were Gentiles. Abraham was not in actuality a Jew, for the Jews are the descendants of Judah, the fourth son of Jacob or Israel. So we see that Rebekah was not an Isrraelite, but a Gentile, so the type holds good.

We must not forget also, that there are "Two Brides" mentioned in the Scriptures. One in the Old Testament and the other in the New. The one in the Old Testament is Israel, the Bride of Jehovah; the one in the New Testament is the Church, the Bride of Christ. Of Israel it is said---"Thy Maker is Thine husband." (Isa. 54: 5-8). Because of her whoredoms, Israel is a cast off WIFE, but God, her husband, promises to take her back when she ceases from her adulteries. (Jer. 3: 1-18; Ez. 16: 1-63; Hosea 2: 1-23; 3: 1-5). She will not be taken back as a **Virgin**, but as a **WIFE**. But it is a **VIRGIN** that the Lamb (Christ) is to marry. So the **WIFE**, who is Israel of the Old Testament cannot be the **BRIDE** or the Virgin of the New Testament. Once more, the **WIFE** who is Israel is to reside in the earthly Jerusalem during the Millennium, while the **BRIDE** (who is the Church) will reside in the New Jerusalem. These distinctions makes it clear that Israel cannot be the "Bride" of Christ. We must remember that John did not call the bride--**WIFE**, until Rev. 21: 9, which was **after the marriage** when she was no longer Bride but **WIFE**.

The Bride of the Lamb is from a disowned and outcast race, made so by the disobedience of the head of that race in the Garden of Eden, but the Bridegroom saw her and loved her. To redeem her He came from His own lovely home in Heaven to her sin-cursed home on earth, where He was rejected by members of her family, and seized and subjected to a mock trial and nailed to a cross as a malefactor, where He laid down voluntarily His life for her, to demonstrate His love, therefore, opening up the way for her redemption from the Law that held her in bondage. He then left her to return to His Father's house to prepare a home for her, and during the period of her engagement He left her with her own family, and simply sending the Holy Spirit to teach and protect her, and fit her for the day of her marriage, when He will descend into midair to meet her on her way to the **BRIDAL HALLS OF HEAVEN**. (I Thess. 4: 16-17).

Many assume that the "Bride" is composed of all the saints from Abel down to the time of the taking out of the Church, but this cannot be so, for the Church did not exist until the Day of Pentecost, and only those who live and die in Christ between Pentecost and the taking out of the Church, belong to the Church.

3. WHERE AND WHEN SHALL THIS MARRIAGE TAKE PLACE?

The Marriage takes place in Heaven after the "Judgment of Reward," and before the appearing of Christ with His Saints at the Revelation.

The character of the ceremony or who shall perform it (no doubt it will be God the Father Himself), and what vows the Bridegroom and Bride will take, is not disclosed, but that there will be a ceremony of some kind that no divorce or separation can break, cannot be questioned, for there never was a legal marriage without some ceremony. Of one thing we are certain that there is no one to give away the Bride, for Christ presents her to Himself a "GLORIOUS CHURCH, not having SPOT, or WRINKLE, or any SUCH THING." (Eph. 5: 25-27).

4. WHAT IS MEANT BY HER MAKING HERSELF READY?

We are told in Rev. 19: 7, that she have "made herself ready," and in verse 8, that it was permitted for her to be "arrayed in fine linen, clean and white; which is the righteousness of the saints," and in chapter Rev. 21: 2, she is described as--- **"prepared as a bride adorned for her husband**."

Remember we are talking about the Church. So where does the Church clothe herself and when? It is a sure thing that she does not clothe herself on earth, for the Bride does not put on her wedding robes until after she has been tried at the Judgment Seat of Christ, where all her "**false works**" will have been consumed by fire (I Cor. 3: 11-15), and it is this "Fiery Judgment" that Peter refers to as the "**TRIAL OF FAITH**" which---"being much more precious than of gold that perisheth, though it be **tried with fire**, might be found unto **praise** and **honor** and **glory** at the **APPEARING OF JESUS CHRIST**." (I Pet. 1: 7). The "**righteousnesses**" of the Saints will be their righteous acts and works that will come out of the "**fiery test**" of the Judgment of Reward, and be found unto **PRAISE** and **HONOR** and **GLORY** at the "**APPEARING**" of Jesus Christ; and these shall make up the beautiful wedding garments in which the Saints shall be clothed. A big different from the "Harlot Wife" of Antichrist, and the spotless white robe of fine linen of the "Bride" of the Lamb.

6. WHAT IS THE MARRIAGE SUPPER?

It is not the wedding itself. The "Marriage Feast" is the supper that follows after the Marriage has been solemnized. It will be such an honor to receive an invitation, and to be present at this affair, that the angel said to John, **"WRITE,"** put it down in black and white before you forget,---**"WRITE, BLESSED ARE THEY WHICH ARE CALLED UNTO THE MARRIAGE SUPPER OF THE LAMB."** What a supper it will be. As a Feast, the Feasts of Belshazzar and Ahasuerus will be but a poor meal in comparison.

7. WHO ARE THE GUESTS?

Once again there is a difference of opinions. It's a sure thing that the Guests **are not the Bride,** at least this is true as to earthly weddings. The Bride would not be "called" or "invited" to her own wedding, she has a place there of her own rights, and there could be no wedding without her. Some hold that the "Virgins" in the parable of the "Ten Virgins" are not the "Bride" but simply "Bridemaids"; and that those invited to the "Marriage Supper" of the King's Son, are simply "Guests" and do not constitute the "Bride." But as both of these Parables do not mention the Bride, and are "Kingdom of Heaven" Parables, which describe the character of this Gospel Dispensation, and have a double significance, we are led to believe that the **"Wise Virgins"** and the Guests who possessed a "Wedding Garment" are intended to represent the BRIDE, because they represent true believers, and true believers constitute the Church, and the Church and the Bride are one and the same.

But there will be "Guests," for as all the dead in Christ shall rise and be present at the "Marriage of the Lamb," and as only those who are saved from Pentecost to the taking out of the Church, belong to the Church which is the Bride, there will be present as "GUESTS" the Old Testament Saints, such as Abel, Seth, Enoch, Noah, Abraham, Job, Moses, David, the Prophets, and even John the Baptist who claimed to be only the "**Friend**" of the Bridegroom. Next will be the "Blood Washed Multitude" that come out of the Tribulation after the Church has been caught out. Then we see that the righteous of all the past Ages and Dispensations, and all the Saints of God who shall be worthy, and who are not included in the Church will be "Guests" at the "Marriage Supper of the Lamb." Angels will be "spectators" of the scene but they cannot be "Guests," for that honor is reserved only for those who have been redeemed by the "Blood of the Lamb."

8. WHAT HAPPENS AFTER THE MARRIAGE SUPPER?

What happens at earthly weddings after the supper? The guests make merry among themselves. Often there is music and dancing, and then the Bridegroom and the Bride change their wedding garments for a travelling dress, and steal away on their wedding trip. Sometimes that trip is a visit to the old home of the Bridegroom or the Bride. So after the "Marriage of the Lamb" the Heavenly Bridegroom will take His Bride on a wedding trip, and to what more suitable place can they go than back to the old home of the Bride, "**This Earth**." The place where the Bridegroom suffered and died to purchase her redemption with His own Blood. The place where her people rejected Him, and despised His Royal claims. Then He will show them that He was no imposter, that He was what He claimed to be, the Son of God. He will then set up His Earthly Kingdom, and the Lord God shall give unto Him the "**THRONE OF DAVID,**" and His Bride (The Church) shall reign with Him for a **THOUSAND YEARS**. Oh what a Beautiful "**HONEY-MOON**" that will be, when, during that long "Millennial Reign" the earth shall be blessed with the presence of the King of Kings and His spouse---**THE**

CHURCH. But that long "Honey-Moon" will end, not for the Bridegroom and the Bride, but for the Earth, by the return of the Bridegroom and the Bride to the Father's House. Then after the Earth has had its "Baptism of Fire," they will return with the descent of the "Holy City" to abide on the "New Earth" forever. John was so enraptured by the revelation that he says---"I fell at the angels feet to worship him. And he said unto me, See thou do it not: I am thy fellow servant, and of thy brethren that have the testimony of Jesus: Worship God: for the Testimony of Jesus is the **SPIRIT OF PROPHECY**." What he is saying is that all prophecy testifies of Jesus.

9. THE BATTLE OF ARMAGEDDON. (REV. 19: 11-19).

In Chapter 6: verse 2, a "White Horse Rider" was seen, who had a bow in his hand, and a crown was given him, and he went forth conquering and to conquer. That "Rider" we saw was "**ANTICHRIST**," but this "Rider" has **eyes like a flame of fire**, and on His head were many crowns, and out of His mouth went a sharp sword. This identifies Him as the person John saw standing in the midst of the "Seven Candlesticks" of Rev. chapter one, and whom we saw to be the "**SON OF MAN**." The name of the first White Horse Rider is not given, but this "White Horse Rider" is called "**THE WORD OF GOD**," and on His Vesture, and on His thigh, a name was written "**KING OF KINGS AND LORD OF LORDS**."

Many stumble at the "**White Horse**" and his **RIDER**; and ask, in amazement, if we believe it? Yes! Why not? We believe it, just as we believe the prophecy of Zech. 9: 9, where the Prophet, speaking of the First coming of Christ, said--- "Behold, thy King cometh unto thee . . . lowly and riding upon an ass, and upon a colt the foal of an ass." Which we know was literally fulfilled as recorded in Matt. 21: 4-11. Jesus, as far as we know, rode but once in the days of His Humiliation, and then upon an humble animal, an ass, but when He comes again in His Glory, as "King of Kings," He shall sit astride a beautiful **WHITE CHARGER**. Oh, you say that is figurative, who ever heard of horses in Heaven? We answer "horses and chariots of fire" were seen in the heavens in the days of Elijah and Elisha, and why not again? II Kings 2: 11; 6: 13-17.

The riders upon these "White Horses" were clothed in fine linen, white and clean. As this is the dress of the Saints that compose the Bride, it is clear that Christ's Bride will accompany Him back to the earth, and here we have the fulfillment of the prophecy of Enoch, the seventh person from adam, recorded in Jude 14----"Behold, the Lord cometh with 10,000 of **HIS SAINTS**." But they will propable be only one division of that great army, for we are told that Christ shall be accompanied by the **ARMIES** of Heaven.

With Christ at this time shall be the "**Overcomers**" of the "Thyatiran Church Period" (A. D. 606-1520), to whom He promised to give power over the nations that they should rule them with a "ROD OF IRON," and to them shall be given some official position of a ruling character.

This fulfills the prophecy of Isa. 11: 1-4, where a colon (:) in verse 4, makes a break or gap that covers this present Dispensation from the First to the Second Coming of Christ---"And He smite the earth with the '**ROD OF HIS MOUTH**,' and with the **BREATH OF HIS LIPS** shall He slay---**THE WICKED** (the **ANTICHRIST**)." II Thess. 2: 7—8. The "**SHARP SWORD**" that goeth out of the mouth of the "White Horse Rider" is not the "**SWORD OF THE SPIRIT**," for that bringeth "Salvation," not destruction, but stands for some supernatural form of destruction, called in the above passage the---"**ROD OF HIS MOUTH.**" Now John saw His VESTURE had been dipped in Blood. So the question is whose blood is this? His own blood that He shed on Calvary, or the blood of His enemies? That this does not refer to Christ's atonement on the Cross is clear, for the Prophet adds---"For the Day of Vengeance is in mine heart, and the year of my redeemed is come." Now there was no "Vengeance" in Christ's heart on the cross. "It was Father forgive them, for they know not what they do."

The time the Prophet foretells, is the "Day of Christ's Vengeance" on His enemies, and the day when He shall redeem His chosen people, the Jews from the power of Antichrist. It is the time when He shall tread---- "THE 'WINEPRESS' OF the Fierceness and Wrath of Almighty God." In Rev. 19: 18 an Angel with a sharp sickle, is told to "Thrust in thy sharp Sickle, and gather the clusters of the 'Vine of the Earth,' for her grapes are fully ripe. We read that "The Winepress was trodden without the City, and blood (not wine), came out of the winepress, even unto the horses' bridles, by the space of a Thousand and Six Hundred Furlongs." We can see that the "Allied Armies" of Antichrist will cover the whole of Palestine, and great shall be the slaughter, that, in the valleys and hollows, all over the whole of Palestine, for the length of Palestine as far south as Bozrah is 1600 furlongs or 200 miles, the blood shall be up to the horses' bridles. It will be the time of which Isaiah speaks, when the land shall be "Soaked with Blood." Isa. 34: 1-8.

The "Tribulation Period" will close with the great "Battle of Amageddon." We have already seen that the armies of the East and the West will be assembled in the Holy Land by the "Demon Spirits" that shall be sent forth from the mouths of the "Satanic Trinity." The field of battle will be the "Valley of Megiddo," located in the heart of Palestine, the battlefield of the great battles of the Old Testament. The forces engaged will be the "Allied Armies" of Antichrist on the one side, and the "Heavenly Army" of Christ on the other side. The "time" will be when the "**Harvest of the Earth**" IS RIPE (Rev. 14: 15), and at the right "Psychological Moment" when the "Allied Armies" of Antichrist are about to take the city of Jerusalem, the Prophet Zechariah says--- "Behold the '**Day of the Lord**' cometh." (The "day of the Lord" is the Millennial Day.) When---"I will Gather All Nations that's against Jerusalem to Battle . . . Then shall the Lord Go Forth and Fight Against Those Nations." (Zech. 14: 1—3).

THIRD DOOM.
"THE BEAST" AND "FALSE PROPHET." (Rev. 19: 20).

The issue of the "Battle of Armageddon" will never be in doubt. The previous summoning of the birds and beasts of prey, prove this. Before the destruction of the army of Antichrist, he and the False Prophet will be cast "alive" into the "Lake of Fire." This shows that they are not "Systems" but "Persons," and as Enoch and Elijah were taken to Heaven without dying, so Antichrist and the False Prophet will be cast into the "Lake of Fire" without dying, and will be still there and alive when Satan is cast in a 1000 years later. This is the culminating act of the "Tribulation Period."

FOURTH DOOM.

THE ANTICHRISTIAN NATIONS. (REV. 19: 21).

So great will be the destruction of human life in the "Battle of Armageddon," that God will prepare for it in advance, to keep the stench of the unburied dead from breeding pestilence.

"And I saw an angel standing in the sun; and he cried with a loud voice, saying to all the fowls that fly in the midst of Heaven (Buzzards, Vultures, Eagles, etc.), Come and gather yourselves together unto the **SUPPER OF THE GREAT GOD**, that ye may eat the flesh of Kings . . . Captains . . Mighty Men, and the flesh of horses and of them that sit on them (common soldiers), and the flesh of all men, both free and bond, both small and great." (Rev. 19: 17, 18).

The words in Rev. 19: 21, "and all the fowls were filled with their flesh," lets us know that those "**Fowl Guests**" will be **GORGED WITH DEAD DECAYING FLESH**. Then will be fulfilled the words of Jesus---"For wheresoever the carcase is, there will the Eagles and birds of prey be gathered together." (Matt. 24: 27-28). The eagle feeds mainly on fresh meat. The Hebrews classed the eagle among the birds of prey, like as the vulture.

The destruction of this great army will be brought about by supernatural means, and as there is to be a "GREAT HAIL" to fall from heaven upon the enemies of God when the "Seventh Vial" is poured out, which includes this period, that may be the means God chooses to use, for it was in that way that the enemies of Israel were destroyed on the same battlefield in the "Battle of Beth-Horon" in the days of Joshua. (Josh. 10: 1-11).

THE INTERVAL BETWEEN THE "FOURTH" AND "FIFTH" DOOMS.

1. SATAN BOUND FOR A THOUSAND YEARS. (REV. 20: 1-3).

In this chapter Satan is called by four different names "Dragon," "Serpent," "Devil," and "Satan." From these and from the fact that he can be bound, we see that he is a "**PERSON**," because you cannot bind an "**influence**" or a "principle of evil." While Satan is the "Prince of the Powers of the Air" (Eph. 2: 2), and the "God of this Age" (II Cor. 4: 4), and the "Ruler of the powers of Darkness" (Eph. 6: 11-12), and that his position is so exalted that even Michael the Archangel dare not to insult him (Jude 9), and while he has great power and influence, yet he is not omnipotent, for One Angel and he is not called a strong angel, is able to seize and bind him. This Angel, who has the "Key" of the "**BOTTOMLESS PIT**," is the same "**STAR Angel**" that is seen by John when the "Fifth Trumpet" sounded (Rev. 9: 1-2), who seems to be the custodian of the "Key" of the "Bottomless Pit."

The objection has been raised to the possibility of binding a "**Spirit**" with an **IRON** chain. But the word "iron" is not used, it is simply a "great chain," and we are told in other scriptures that "Spirit" beings can be chained. In II Pet. 2: 4, and Jude 6, we read of the angels who sinned and Kept not their "First Estate," and who are now "**reserved in CHAINS**," **in darkness,** unto the judgment of the great Day which is (the Great "White Throne" Judgment).

The binding of Satan reveals the fact that God can stop his work when ever He is ready, and that without sending the armies of Heaven to do so. When the time has come, God will empower and command a **single Angel** to seize, handcuff, and imprison him, just as an officer of the law with a warrant arrests and locks up a criminal. Satan is not cast at this time into the "Lake of Fire," to keep company with the "Beast" and "False Prophet," because God has further use for him at the end of the 1000 years for which period he is bound.

2. THE FIRST RESURRECTION (REV. 20: 4-6).

In this chapter we meet for the first time the expression---"**THE FIRST RESURRECTION.**" In I Thess. 4: 16, we read that the dead in Christ shall rise First, but as no wicked are mentioned it is simply a relative ststement to show that the living Christians shall not be caught away before the "Dead in Christ" shall be raised. These verses speaks of two separate "Companies of Believers" who are to be raised, each in their own order, at the "First Resurrection."

The First Company is described by the words---"I saw Thrones, and they sat upon them, and Judgment was given unto them." Now the only "Company of Believers" that we see sitting on Thrones are the "Four and Twenty Elders" of Rev. 4: 4-5. These stand for the Church, and were resurrected or caught out before "The Tribulation," and are the "**Harvest**" of which Christ and those who rose at the time of His Resurrection, were the "**First Fruits**."

The Second Company is described by the words--- "And I saw the **SOULS** of them that were **beheaded for the witness of Jesus**, and for the word of God, and which had not **worshipped the 'Beast,' neither his 'Image,' neither had received his 'Mark' upon their foreheads, or in their hands**." This company is made up of those who were slain for refusing to worship the "Beast" or his "Image," and represent the "**Tribulation Saints**," or those that perish as martyrs after the Church has been caught out, and during the "Tribulation Period," and are the "**Gleanings**" of the "Harvest."

Now it also states that these Two Companies "Lived," in that they were dead but lived again, after they will have been raised **from the dead,** Because John saw the Tribulation Saints in their disembodied state between death and the resurrection of the body. This shows us that both these Companies were resurrected and lived and were to reign with Christ for **a 1000 YEARS**, not just the Tribulation Saints but both Companies makes up the **FIRST RESURRECTION SAINTS**.

In Rev. 20: 5, we have another class or company of persons mentioned, and they are called the "**REST OF THE DEAD**," Who are not to live again until the 1000 years are finished. It is clear that there are to be two Resurrrections of the dead, the first of the "**RIGHTEOUS**," and the second of the "**WICKED**," and that these two Resurrections are to be **1000 YEARS APART**.

But we do not have to depend on this passage to prove that the "Righteous" shall rise before the "Wicked," its value lies in the fact that it gives us the **LENGTH OF TIME** (1000 years) between the Two Resurrections. Now the Scriptures, while they speak of the Resurrections of the "**JUST**" and the "**UNJUST**" (Act 24: 15) and a resurrection of "LIFE," and a Resurrection of "DAMNATION" (John 5: 28-29), also speak of an "**OUT**" Resurrection "**FROM AMONG**" the dead, called in Luke 14: 13-14, the Resurrection of the "**JUST**." Now in Luke 20: 35-36 there is a Resurrection spoken of called a Resurrection "**FROM THE DEAD**," (out from) and is an "OUT" Resurrection, because those who rise are called the "**CHILDREN OF GOD**," being the children of "**THE RESURRECTION**," (or out from) and again in Heb. 11: 35, we read of a "**BETTER RESURRECTION**," and all these references to a "**SPECIAL**" resurrection are made clear, and the **"time element"** and its "**length**" (1000 years) between the resurrection of the "**JUST**" and "**UNJUST**" revealed in the passage that we are considering; there could be no statement more clearer than----"**THE REST OF THE DEAD LIVED NOT AGAIN UNTIL THE THOUSAND YEARS WERE FINISHED**," to show that the "**Unrighteous Dead**" will not be raised until the **end of the Millennium**. This at one stroke does away with the argument of those who claim that all the dead will be raised at the beginning of the Millennium, and shall have another chance to accept the Gospel and be saved.

We read---"Blessed and holy is he that hath part in the '**First Resurrection**'; on such the '**SECOND DEATH**' have no power." What is the "**Second Death**"? First, what is **DEATH**? It is the separation of the "soul" and "spirit" from the "body." That is the "**FIRST DEATH**." At the Resurrection the "soul" and "spirit" are reunited to the "body." This is true of both the Righteous and the wicked. But the wicked after they have been raised are to be judged at the Great White Throne Judgment, and because their names are not found written in the "Book of Life," they are sentenced to die again, that is their "soul" and "spirit" are again separated from their body, and they go to the "LAKE OF FIRE" without a material body, and as "soul" and "spirit" are incombustible they can remain in the flames of a literal fire for all eternity without being consumed. This is the doom of the wicked dead. The Rich Man in Hell (Luke 16: 19-31) was conscious and tormented in the flame after his death, and he shall remain so until his body ahall be raised from the dead at the Resurrection of the wicked, and when he shall be judged and condemned at the Great White Throne Judgment, and sentenced to die again, his "soul" and "spirit" will descend to the "Lake of Fire" (the Final Hell), where they will exist in a conscious state and in torment for all eternity. But the "Second Death" has no terror for the Righteous, for the promise is that it shall have no power over them.

3. THE MILLENNIUM. (REV. 20: 4).

That there is to be a period of a 1000 years during which Satan shall be bound and Christ shall reign on this earth, is plainly stated in the New Testament. This period is mentioned six times in Rev. 20: 1-7, and is generally called "The Millennium," from the Latin words "Mille" which means "1000," and "Annum" which means "year." It is to be regretted, however, that the word "Millennium" Could ever move with aglity the Biblical word "Kingdom," for it is in this period that

Christ taught His Disciples to pray for in the petition --- "Thy Kingdom Come."

As we move forward, let us drop for the present, the word "Millennium" and look at the word "Kingdom." In the book of Daniel, we learn that there were to be "Four World-wide Kingdoms" that were to succeed each other on the earth and that they were to be destroyed in turn by a Kingdom called the "Stone Kingdom."

As those "Four Kingdoms" were "Literal" Kingdoms it followsthat the "Stone Kingdom" must be a "Literal" Kingdom, forit takes the place of those Kingdoms and "fills the whole earth." Therefore, this "Stone Kingdom" must be the "Millennial Kingdom of Christ."

The time when this "Stone Kingdom" shall be set up is at the "Revelation of Christ," When He shall come with the "armies of Heaven" and destroy Antichrist (Rev. 19: 11-21) and judge the Nations. And before Him shall be gathered all nations; and He shall separate them one from another as a shepherd divideth his sheep from the goats, (Goat Nations) on the left. Then shall the King say unto them on His right hand, Come, ye blessed of my Father. Inherit the **Kingdom Prepared for you from the Foundation of the World**." (Matt. 25: 31-34). This Kingdom is an earthly, visible Kingdom, and is the "Millennial Kingdom" of the Lord Jesus Christ.

Now the **Form of Government** will be a "Theocracy," God will rule in the person of the Lord Jesus Christ. (Luke 1: 30-33). After reading this message, you will see that there are 7 of God's "**shalls**" included in the passage. Four of them have been fulfilled, for Mary did bring forth a "son," He was called "Jesus," He was "great," and was called the "Son of the Highest"; the other three fulfillments is yet to come.

Whether Christ shall sit in person on the Throne at Jerusalem, or whether He shall rule through another is not so clear. There are serveral passages of Scripturs that seem to teach that King David will be raised and placed on the throne again, and that the Children of Israel will seek him; or it may mean that the new King shall be named David. (Hosea 3:5; Jer. 30: 9; Ezek. 37: 24, 25.; 34: 24).

As the "Lord of Hosts" shall reign in Mt. Zion, and in Jerusalem, and before His ancients "gloriously" (Isa. 24: 23), it is believed that King David willreign simply as "Regent," and will be called "King" or "Prince" as circumstances may require. It is very clear from Ezekiel that the "Prince," whoever he may be, is not perfect, and has to offer sacrifices for himself. (Ezek. 45: 22).

The promise that Jesus made to His Disciples in Matt. 19: 28, "that they shall sit upon Twelve Thrones, Judging the Twelve Tribes of Israel." in all probability does not refer to the "Millennial Age," but to the "Perfect Age," the "Age" that is to follow the renovation of the Earth by fire. The use of the word "regeneration" suggests this, as it refers to the time when the present earth is to be "re-created" and made "New."

We must remember that angels appeared in human form and "ate" and "drink" with men in Old Testament times. (Gen. 18: 1-8). Also we must not forget that they who shall be accounted worthy to obtain "That Age," and the "**Resurrection From Among the Dead**," shall be "**Angel like**" (Luke 20: 35, 36), and like the angels they can mingle with earth's inhabitants, their visible bodily forms, can eat and drink, and there is probably more truth in the Prophet's utterance that in those days, "They that wait upon the Lord shall renew their strength; they shall mount up with wings as eagles (Angels); they shall run and not be weary; they shall walk and not faint." (Isa. 40: 31). This can be said of only those who have been "Raised in Power." (I Cor. 15: 42, 43).

The Seat of Government will be in Jerusalem. However, Jerusalem is to be trodden down by the Gentiles, until the "Times of the Gentiles be fulfilled." Then it will be rebuilt. The "Royal Grant of land that God gave to Abraham and his descendants extended from the "River of Egypt" unto the "Great river Euphrates." (Gen 15: 18). This "Royal Grant" was not conditional and was never revoked. It is 8 times as large as that formerly occupied by the Twelve Tribes.

This "Royal Grant" is to be divided among the restored Twelve Tribes in paralled horizontal sections, beginning at Hamath on the North with a section for Dan, next will come Asher, then Naphtali, Manassah, Ephraim, Reuben and Judah. Then comes the "**Holy Oblation**," a square tract on the west of Jordan, 50 miles on a side. South of the "Holy Oblation" will be the Tribe of Benjamin, Simeon, Issachar, Zebulon and Gad. The "Holy Oblation" is divided into three horizontal sections. The Northen section is 50 miles long from East to West, and about 20 miles wide. It is called the "Levites' Portion." South of it is the "Priests' Portions" of equal size. South of the "Priests' Portion" is the section for the "City" with its suburbs and farming sections. This section is 50 miles long, from East to West, and 5 miles wide (Ezek. 48: 15-19). The City of Jerusalem is located in the centre of this section. This will help to map out the whole of the "Holy Oblation," as the "New City" (Jerusalem) is to be located on the site of the Old. The "New City," however, is to be much larger than the Old. It is to be 9 miles square, along with its suburbs, ½ mile on a side, 10 miles square. It will have a wall around it with 3 gates on each side like the New Jerusalem (Ezek. 48: 30-35), These gates will be named after the 12 sons of Jacob.

The "Sanctuary," will not be rebuilt in the "New City," but in the "Middle" of the "Holy Oblation." (Ezek. 48: 10, 20, 21). This will locate it at or near Shiloh, where the Tabernacle rested after the Children of Israel conquered the Land, and where it remainded until the Temple of Solomon was finished. A "Highway" shall be from the "Sanctuary" to the "New City." (Isa. 35: 8). It will be A magnificently beautiful boulevard, 12 miles long, lined with beautiful shade trees. The "New Temple" or Sanctury will occupy a space of nearly a square mile. The old Temple was not even a mile in circuit. (Ezek. 42: 15-20).

The size of the "New City," the location of the "New Sanctuary" and the elevation of the Dead Sea, which is now 1200 feet below the level of the Mediterranean Sea, call for great physical changes in the land surface of Palestine. How are these changes to come about?

When Christ comes back it will be to the Mount of Olives from whence He went up. (Acts 1: 9-12). The Prophet Zechariah describes what will then happen in Zech. 14: 4, 10, 11. These changes will probably be brought about by earthquakes or volcanic action. (Micah. 1: 3, 4). These great physical changes will level the land surface of Palestine, and make room for the "New City," and raise the Dead Sea, so its waters can flow into both the Red Sea and the Mediterranean Sea. Ezekiel tells us that the name of Jerusalem in that day shall be "**Jehovah-Shammah**," **the Lord Is There**. (Ezek. 48: 35).

As we have seen **The Temple and its Worship** will be located in the centre of the "Holy Oblation." A full description of the Temple and its courts is given in Ezek. 40: 1; 44: 31. No such building as Ezekiel so minutely describes has ever yet been built, and so the prophecy cannot refer to either Zerubbabel's or Herod's Temple, and as there is to be no Temple in the New Jerusalem, it must be a description of the Temple that is to be on the earth during the Millennium. That it does not belong to the New Earth is also clear, for the land in which it is located is bounded by the Sea, and the waters that flow from it, flow "into the Sea," but in the New Earth there is "no more sea." (Rev. 21: 1). This is still further confirmed by the Prophet's mention of the "desert," the "River Jordan," the "Mediterranean Sea," and other locatities that will not be found on the New Earth after its renovation by fire. The New Temple, will lack many things that were the features of the old Temple. There will be no "Ark of the Covenant," no "Pot of Manna," no "Aaron's Rod" to bud, no "Table of the Law," no "Cherubim," no "Mercy Seat," no "Golden Candlestick," no "Shew Bread," no "Altar of Incense," no "Veil," no unapproachable "Holy of Holies" where the High Priest alone might enter, nor is there any "High Priest" to offer atonement for sin, or to make intercession for the people, However, there is a rather obscure passage in Zech. 6: 12, 13 that means that Christ (The Branch, Jer. 23: 5, 6) shall be a "King-Priest," and perform the duties of High Priest along with His Kingly office. There shall be a daily "morning" sacrifice, but no evening sacrifice. (Ezek. 46: 13-15). The offerings will be the "Burnt," the "Meat," the "Drink," the "Sin," the "Peace" (Ezek. 45: 17), and the "Trespass" offering. (Ezek. 42: 13). Two Feasts are to be observed, "The Passover," but no Passover Lamb will be offered as Jesus fulfilled that Type (Ezek. 45: 21-24), and the "Feast of Tabernacles," (Zech. 14: 16-19). This Feast is to be observed by all the nations, under penalty of "Drought" or "Plague."

The "Feast of Pentecost" will be done away with on account of its fulfillment. The "Day of Pentecost," recorded in Acts 2: 1-4, was only a partial fulfillment of the prophecy of Joel 2: 28-32. No such wonders in the heavens and the earth as "blood," and "fire" and "pillars of smoke." The "Sun turned to darkness," and the "Moon into blood," occurred at Pentecost. But all those things will happen before "The Great and Terrible Day of the Lord."

The conversion of the Jewish Nation will be sealed with a great outpouring of the Holy Spirit. The original prophecy in Joel was given to Israel, and its partial fulfillment at Pentecost seems to have been limited to Israel. The knowledge of the Lord, however, will be world-wide, and "it shall come to pass that ten men of all languages and nations shall take hold of the skirt of him that is a **Jew**, saying **we will go with you; for we have heard that God is with you**." (Zech. 8: 22, 23). There will be one "universal religion" in that day. (Malachi 1: 11). The "Shekinah Glory" that departed from the Temple at the time of the Babylonian Captivity (Ezek. 10: 18-20; 11: 22, 23), will again take up its residence in the "New Temple." (Ezek. 43: 1-5).

THE CHARACTER OF THE MILLENNIUM.
Satan bound. (Rev. 20: 1-3).

That man may be "without excuse" God is going to subject him to a final test under the most favorable circumstances. Man has charged his fall and continuance in sin to Satan. "Take him away," man cries, "paralyze his power; cripple his malignant activity; bind and imprison him and deliver us from his dominating influence, and then you will see that man is radically good and virtuous and is simply the victim of an unfavorable environment."

God answers it shall be done. Satan shall be bound and imprisoned so that he can no longer deceive men, lest man shall say that sinful habits are too deeply rooted to be so soon eradicated, the test shall last for a **thousand years**, and man shall have during that period of probation all the blessed influences of the **Holy Spirit** and the presence of **Christ Himself.**

Man has never known and therefore cannot conceive what this world would be like free from Satanic influence. It would certainly be a marvelously different world. There would be no one to stir up hate and passion, and engender strife and turmoil. True, man would still have an evil heart of unbelief to contend against, but it would be like a magazine of gunpowder without a spark to ignite it. That the evil heart of man has not been eradicated will be evident when at the close of the Millennium, Satan is loosed and finds no difficulty in deceiving the nations. (Rev. 20: 8).

During the Millennium the "Prince of Peace" "enthroned." When the "Great Red Dragon" (Satan) is cast out of the Heavenlies there will be cast out with him all the "Principalities and Powers" and "Age Rulers of Darkness" (Eph. 6: 12), and the Heavens which now are "not clean" in His sight (Job 15: 15), will be "cleansed" of all evil powers.

There wll be no universal peace until the Lord comes back. Then the nations will beat their swords into "plow-shares" and their spears into "pruning-hooks" (Mich. 4: 3, 4), and shall be no longer impoverished by the enormous tax on their revenues for the support of armies and navies and the building of heavily armed battleships. Then ships of war and armorclad vessels will rust and rot in the navy yards and guns and cannons will be recast into implements of agriculture. The great armies of earth will be disbanded, and in the pursuits of peace and the tilling of the soil, the depleted treasuries of the world will be replenished. There will be little if any political graft. There will be no entailed estates if the law of the "Year of Jubilee" is re-established. (Lev. 25: 8-17; Num. 36: 4).

THE REVIVAL OF THE LAND OF PALASTINE.

The Land of Palestine when it was first occupied by the Children of Israel under the leader-ship of Joshua, was a land of "Milk" and "Honey" and of "all manner of fruits," and its soil brought forth "abundantly," and this continued as long as the Children of Israel kept its Sabbaths. But God had warned them that if they did not obey Him and turned aside to worship other gods He would shut up the heavens and the harvests would fail. (Deut. 11: 13-17). Palestine today has the same fertile soil it had in Joshua's time, but it lacks rain and irrigation. God has withheld the "early" and "latter" rain, to some degree, but they are now becoming more frequent and copious. Soil in the Palestinian-Israel case is the best example where water conflict is still causing problems; a set of targets was agreed upon for the year 2015.

In the Millennium the Land of Palestine will be restored to its former fertility. This will be aided not only by the rains, but by numerous rivers and streams that shall flow from the "New River" that shall have its source in the Sanctuary. (Joel 3: 18).

The "Mountain dropping new wine," and the "hills flowing with milk," are figures of speech declaring that the mountain sides will be covered with vineyards from which an abundance of wine shall be obtained, and that the pasture lands will be so productive that they will sustain vast herds of milk cattle. The harvests will be so great and abundant that the ploughman will "overtake the reaper," and the treader of grapes, him that "soweth seed." (Amos 9: 13). (Isa. 35: 1; 55: 13; Psa. 67: 6; Joel 2: 24-26).

CHANGES IN THE ANIMAL KINGDOM. (ISA. 11: 6-9).

We cannot spiritualize these words. This was the character of these animals in Eden before the fall, and in the Ark. The ferocity of the brute creation is the outcome of the "Fall of Man." While the context seems to imply that this change in the brute creation has reference to the "Millennial Earth," where as it may be partially true, yet the fact that the Edenic condition of the earth is not to be restored until the appearance of the New Earth may postpone the fulfillment of the prophecy until then. The Apostle Paul says in Rom. 8: 23, "We know that the **Whole Creation** groaneth and travaileth in pain together until now. . . . Waiting for the adoption to wit, the **Redemption of Our Body**." In other words, until the human race is redeemed from the results of the "Fall, and fitted to occupy the New Earth, Creation must wait for its restoration to 'Edenic conditions'."

HUMAN LIFE WILL BE PROLONGED.

"There shall be no more from there an infant of days, for the child shall die a hundred years old or older." (Isa. 65: 20). For a person dying 100 years old shall be considered only a child. Therefore a man, to be called a man, must live for several hundred years. For Isaiah says in Isa. 65: 22, "that as the days of a tree (oak tree) so are the days of my people."

Patriarchal years will be restred, and men shall live as long as they did before the flood. This may be due to some climatic or atmospheric change, or to the healing or life-giving qualities of the water of the "New River" that shall flow from the "Sanctuary," and the leaves of the trees that line the banks of the River, which shall be for "Medicine." (Ezek. 47: 12).

THERE WILL BE A SEVENFOLD INCREASE OF LIGHT.

Isaiah said in Isa. 30: 26 that "even the light of the moon shall be as the light of the sun, and the light of the sun shall be **SEVENFOLD** as the light of seven days, in the day that the Lord bindeth up the disruption of His people, and healeth the stroke of their wound." The "atmosphere" of the Millennial Earth will be of such a character as to make moonlight nights as bright as day, and the days seven times as bright.

(Isa. 60: 19-20) Refers to that part of the Holy Land that shall be illuminated by the "Shekinah Glory," where it will make no difference whether the sun shines or not. It will have its complete fulfillment when the nations of the New Earth shall walk in the Light of the **New Jerusalem**. (Rev. 21: 23,24).

Israel's Mission during the "Millennial Age" will be that of "blessing" to the Gentile nations. Of the nation of Israel, that has never as yet been a leading nation. God says in Deu. 28: 13, "I will make thee the **Head**, and not the **Tail**." The nations today (21st century) are a "Headless" body. There is no "Chief Nation" today. In that day Israel shall be the "Chief Nation," and the nation that will not serve her shall perish. (Isa. 60: 12).

But those nations will only be keap in subjection by the "Iron Rule" of Christ. This is brought out in the "Messianie Psalm," (Psa. 2: 6-9). It is very clear that during the "Millennial Age" the "will of God" will not be done on earth as it is done in heaven. The peace among the nations will be more superficial than real. It will only be feigned obedience, more the result of fear =than of love. As the "afternoon" of that long "Millennial Day" draws to a close the shadows deepen.

4. SATAN LOOSED. (REV. 20: 7-8).

As the evening shadows of the Millennial Day fall, the Angel who imprisoned Satan will unlock the "prison house" of the "Bottomless Pit," and Satan will come forth embittered by his forced confinement to vent his anger upon the people of God, a refutation of the claim that the miseries of perdition will lead to repentance. Satan will still be the same malignant being after his 1000 years of confinement that he was before. His hatred against God and His people will be unquenched.

FIFTH DOOM.
GOG AND MAGOG.

As soon as Satan is loosed from his prison in the "Bottomless Pit," he will find a vast multitude ready to believe his lie, and to serve and obey him. He will gather them from the "**Four Quarters of the Earth**" to battle. They will be in number as the "**sand of the sea**." (Rev. 20: 8-9). The revolt will be worldwide, and will mean the **Mobilizing of Vast Armies**. Satan will conduct them across the "**Breadth of the Earth**" until they circle around the entire "Camp of the Saints" or (the Holy Land), and lay siege once more to the "**Beloved City**." We now see that the unregenerated heart is like a powder magazine, all it needs is a match to set it off, and Satan when freed will be that match. This, the "**last war**" that this world will ever see, will be bloodless, for the vast armies of Satan shall be destroyed by **FIRE**.

From this we see that the "Millennial Dispensation," like the six Dispensations before it, will end in failure. God will have tested man in "Innocence," under "Conscience," under "Self-Government," under the "Headship of the Family," under "Law," under "Grace," and finally under the influence of the "Holy Spirit," free from Satanic influences, and under them all he will prove himself to be hopelessly, incurably bad.

If after a 1000 years of the Presence of the Lord, and of universal peace and blessing, man still persists in rebelling against his Maker, what will there be left for God to do to or for us? Humanly speaking, there will seem to be nothing for God to do but destroy the human race. To send another Flood and wipe out mankind. But this He cannot do, for He promised Noah that He would never again destroy the earth with a flood of waters. (Gen. 9: 11). But do something He must, so He decides to purge the earth with Fire. (II Pet. 3: 7).

SIXTH DOOM.

SATAN. (REV. 20: 10).

As punishment for his final act of Rebellion, Satan shall be seized, and hurled into the "**LAKE OF FIRE**," where he will find alive and waiting for him the "**Beast**" and the "**False Prophet**" who were cast there a 1000 years before. The "Lake of Fire" was prepared for the Devil and his angels (Matt. 25: 41), not to consume them in, for God could do that with **fire from heaven**, but to **PUNISH THEM IN**; and all those whose names are not written in the "Book of Life" will go to the same place to spend eternity. The reason why Satan does not want people to read and study the Book of Revelation is, because he does not want the world to know that there is to be an end to his power. Only the "**bodies**" of those who perish in this last great war will be destroyed by fire, their "**souls**" and "**spirits**" will go to the "Hell Compartment" of the "Underworld" to come out at the Resurrection of the dead and appear at the "Great White Throne Judgment," and be sentenced to the "**SECOND DEATH**," which as we have seen, means that they must spend eternity without a material body in the "Lake of Fire."

SEVENTH DOOM. THE WICKED DEAD.

"THE GREAT WHITE THRONE JUDGMENT." (REV. 20: 11-15).

This is not a "**General Judgment**," for there is no such thing in the scriptures. The Church is not in this Judgment, nor is Israel, for both have been already judged. The Church was Judged at the "**Judgment Seat of Christ**," and Israel was judged during the "**Tribulation Period**." This is a Judgment of the **DEAD ONLY**, and is different from the Judgment of "**The Nations**" recorded in Matt. 25: 31-46. That is on the earth, this is in Heaven. That is of the "**Living Nations**," this is of the

DEAD. In other words for the Nations' treatment of Christ's brethren, the Jews, this is for **WORKS**. There no books are opened, here they are. No "**Book of Life**" is mentioned there, here there is. That Judgment was before the Millennium, when Christ shall sit on the "**Throne of His Glory**," and is to find out what Nations shall have a right to enter into the "Millennial Kingdom," this is after the Millennium when Christ shall sit on the "**Great White Throne**." The two Judgment are entirely separate as to time, place, basis of judgment and result.

In this Judgment "**Death**" and "**Hell**" are perfect examples. By "**Death**" we are to understand the "**Grave**" which holds the "**body**" until the Resurrection; by "**Hell**," the Compartment of the "**Underworld**" or "**HADES**," where the "**souls**" of the Wicked Dead remain until the Resurrection of the Wicked. That both "**Death**" and "**Hell**" are cast into the "**LAKE OF FIRE**" signifies that Death and Sin will not be found on the New Earth.

The "Great White Throne" will not be on the earth, for the "Great White Throne Judgment" will take place during the "Renovation of the Earth by Fire," for the "Renovation of the Earth" is reserved or kept until the time of that Judgment which Peter calls "**The Day of Judgment and Perdition of Ungodly Men**" (II Pet. 3: 7). Because the Judgment of the "Great White Throne" is the Judgment of the **WICKED DEAD**. Now the words---"Whosoever was not found written in the '**Book of Life**'," implies that there will be **some**, probably very few in comparison, who are Righteous at the "Second Resurrection." At the close of the Millennium, and just before the "Renovation of the Earth By Fire," the living Righteous will probably be translated, and the living Wicked or Ungodly will be destroyed in the flames that will consume the Earth's atmosphere and exterior surface.

The Wicked or Ungodly will not be judged to see whether they are entitled to "Eternal Life," but to ascertain the "degree" of their punishment. The sad feature of this Judgment will be that there will be many kind and lovable people there who were not saved, and who will be classed among the "ungodly" because they rejected Christ as a Saviour. The "Books" will be opened in which the "Recording Angel" has kept a record of every person's life, and they will be Judged every man **according to his "Work**s." The worst of all is, that those who were not so bad must spend Eternity with the ungodly, and that is in the "Lake of Fire." Their punishment includes the "Second Death," which means, that they shall lose their resurrection body, in which they were judged and become "**disembodied spirits**" again, and so exist in the "**Lake of Fire**" **FOREVER**.

There in the "**Lake of Fire**" will be Cain and the wicked Antediluvians; the inhabitants of Sodom and Gomorrah; Pharoah, Ahab, Jezebel, Judas and all those Scribes and Pharisees and Chief Priests who caused the Crucifixion of our Lord, and did not repent, and Ananias and Sapphira, and the great host of the wicked and rejectors of Christ of all nations and ages.

The "**Fallen Angels**" who are "**reserved in everlasting chains under darkness**," will be Judged at this time, which **Jude** calls the "**Judgment of the GREAT DAY**." (Jude 6). When this Judgment is over the Devil and his angels, and all the ungodly, will have been consigned to the "Lake of Fire," and the Universe purged of all evil, and righteousness shall reign supreme on the New Earth.

THE SEVEN NEW THINGS

----

1. THE NEW HEAVEN (REV 21: 1).

As the word **HEAVEN** is here, and in Gen. 1: 1, in the singular number, it will clarify matters to limit this creative act to our own planet, rather than the whole of the sidereal heavens, or the starry spaces of the Universe. By a new heaven then we are to understand a new atmosphere for the new earth

2. THE NEW EARTH. (REV. 21: 1-8).

The first heaven and the first earth were created in the dateless past. The Scriptures begin with the sublime declaration---"In the beginning God **CREATED** the heaven and the earth." (Gen. 1: 1), The second verse of Gen. 1, records that "the earth was without form and void; and darkness was upon the face of the deep." Now this earth was not originally created "**formless and void,**" according to Isa. 45: 18 "Thus said the Lord that created the heavens; He is God; that formed the earth and made it; He established it, He created it not a waste, He formed it to be inhabited." Read Jer. 4: 23-26. What caused the earth to become a waste after its original creation is not expressly stated. Some awful catastrophe must have befallen it. It is clear from the account of the fall of Adam and Eve that sin existed before man was created. The inference is from Ezek. 28: 12-19, and Isa. 14: 12-14, that when the earth was originally created that Satan was placed in charge of it, and that he and his angels rebelled and led astray the inhabitants of the Original Earth, and that the Pre-Adamite race are now the demons who as they are permitted liberty seek to re-embody themselves in human beings that they may again dwell on the earth. It is clear that the Original Earth was inhabited, or God would not have blessed Adam and Eve and said---"Be fruitful and multiply and **REPLENISH the Earth**." (Gen. 1: 28). It does not follow however that those inhabitants were human beings like ourselves. No human remains have ever been found ante-dating the creation of man.

There can be no question that the Earth in its original formation required millions of years. There is ample time in the statement of Gen. 1: 1 that---"In the BEGINNING God 'created' the heaven and the earth," for all the "Geologic Ages" that science declares were necessary for the creation of the Earth. There is no conflict between the Bible and Science as to the time occupied in the formation of the Earth.

How long a period elapsed between the Creation of the Earth and its becoming "**formless and void**" we do not know, neither do we know how long it continued in that condition, but what we do know, is that when the time came in the purpose of God to bring it to a habitable state, and make it fit for the abode of the human race, He did it in six periods of longer or shorter duration. These "Periods" were Six in number, and with the seventh or Sabbatic Period, are called the "**Creative Week**."

These "Six Periods" do not describe or include the original creation. For the word "**CREATE**" is not mentioned after Gen. 1: 1 until verse 21, which describes the work of the Fifth Day. God did not "create light" on the First Day. He simply said ---"**let there be light**," as one would say "**turn on the light**."

On the Second Day God simply divided the waters by providing clouds to hold the moisture of the atmosphere.

The word of the Third Day is "**twofold**," the separation of the land from the sea, and the reappearance of vegetable life. This was not a new creation but a **RESURRECTION**. The earth rises up out of the "**Waters of Death**," and seeds, and the roots of plants and herbs are called upon to germinate and sprout and grow as they did before the catastrophe that submerged the Primeval Earth. If that catastrophe was what we know as the "Glacial Period" the resurrection of plant life no more required a "**creative act**" than vegetation does in the spring of the year after the winter is over. This is clear, for when we read Gen. 1: 11-12 where it says, "Let the earth bring forth grass, the herb yielding seed, and the fruit tree yielding fruit after its kind, whose seed is in itself, in the earth." However, the seed was already in the earth, having been buried by the flood that swept over the Primeval Earth, and, being indestructible, it only needed the proper condition to spring up and cover the earth with verdure. This reveals the fact that the Primeval Earth was clothed with verdure, and covered with plants and trees.

The appearance of the Sun and the moon on the fourth Day was not a new creation. They had existed in connection with the Primeval Earth and had not been destroyed when it was made waste. The word translated "made" in the 16th verse of Gen. 1, is not the same word as is translated "created" in verse one of Gen. 1, and does not imply a "**creative act**." What is meant is that the clouds broke away that up to this time had shrouded the earth and permitted the Sun and Moon to be seen, and that from that time they were appointed to measure the days, and years, and seasons as we have them today. In other words, on the Fourth Day "**Time**" in contrast with "**eternity**" began.

The work of the Fifth Day was the "**CREATION**" of fish and fowl. Here is the first time we come across the word "**create**" since we read of the original creation of the Earth in verse 1 of Gen. 1. This shows that all "animal life" was destroyed in the catastrophe that overtook the Primeval Earth. We have traces of this animal life in the fossil remains of birds and animals found in the earth. If scientists will relegate fossils and the remains of mammoth animals, etc., to the period of the Primeval Earth there will be no conflict between Science and the Genesis account of Creation. The remains of man are never found in a "fossil state," showing that man did not exist on the Primeval Earth. Man was made for this present earth and is a "NEW" Creation.

The creative work of the Sixth Day was "twofold," that of land animals and man. These land animals were probably the same that we have today. The fact that they were created "**after their kind**," which expressions is six times repeated, shows that they were not "**evolved**" from one common species. That man also was "**CREATED**" as man, shows that he has not descended from an "**ape**." Man was made in the "**IMAGE OF GOD**," and not in the image of an "**ape**," and was not formed from a brute, but of the "Dust of the Earth." The fact is, there is an "IMPASSABLE GULF" between the lowest order of man and the highest type of beast that science has failed to bridge. The "**Missing Link**" has never been found.

That all the different species of animals were created "separately" is proven from the fact that when species are crossed their offspring are **sterile**. The crossing of the jackass and a mare is the mule, and a mule is a hybrid and is **sterile**. That the whole human race is of "**one species**" and had a common origin (Acts 17: 26) is clear from the fact that, when the different races of the earth's inhabitants marry their offspring are not sterile but fertile. This nullifies the argument that the white race alone is the Adamic race. It should also make it clear that Adam was created from the dust of the ground (Gen. 2: 7) and according to science that area was in that part of Africa that is now called Egypt, and the dust of the ground had to be tan or light brown in color at that time. Therefore, Adam's complection had to be "**Tan or Light Brown.**"

Neither was Adam created a baby or a primitive savage, but a full grown man, perfect in intellect and knowledge, else he could not have named the beasts of the field and the fowls of the air. And the fact that his descendants had such skill in the invention of musical instruments and mechanical devices and could build cities and towers and such a vessel as the Ark, proves that the men of Antediluvian times were men of gigantic intellect and attainments, and that instead of man having "**evolved upward**" he has "**degenerated downward**."

THE NEW HEAVEN AND THE NEW EARTH.

Immediately after the destruction of Satan and his armies, John says in Rev. 20: 11.

"I saw a 'Great White Throne' and Him that sit on it, from whose face the **Earth** and the **Heaven** (atmosphere of the earth) **fled away**; and there was no place for them."

John then describes the Judgment of the "Great White Throne," and then adds---

"I saw a New Heaven; and a New Earth; for the first heaven and the first earth were passed away; and there was no more sea." (Rev. 21: 1).

We are not ignorant of such a change in this earth, but John does not tell us how it will come to pass. But the Apostle Peter does.

"But the heavens and the earth which are now, by the same word are kept in store, **RESERVED UNTO FIRE** aginst the **Day of Judgment and Perdition of Ungodly Men**. (The Great White Throne Judgment)—The 'Day of the Lord' will come as a thief in the night; and the **Heavens shall Pass Away With a Great Noise**, and the **Elements Shall Melt With Fervent Heat, the Earth Also and the Words That Are Therein Shall be Burned Up**."

"Nevertheless we, according to His Promise in (Isa. 65: 17; 66: 22) shall look for a New Heaven and a New Earth, wherein dwelleth righteousness." (II Pet. 3: 7-13).

It appears that Peter is referring to the same event as John, for he says it is to be at the "**Day of Judgment and Perdition of Ungodly Men**," and that is the "**Great White Throne Judgment**" of the **Wicked Dead**.

However, A reading on the surface of the above passage would lead us to believe that the earth as a planet, and the sidereal heavens, are to be **destroyed by fire and pass away**. But a careful study of the Scriptures will show us that this is not so, that what is to happen is, that this present earth, and the atmosphere surrounding it, is to be Renovated by fire, so that its exterior surface shall be completely changed, and all that sin has brought into existence, such as thorns and thistles, disease germs, insect pests, ect., shall bee destroyed, and the atmosphere purified and forever freed from evil spirits and destructive agencies.

That this is the correct view of the passage is clear from Peter's words in II Pet. 3: 5-6.

"By the word of God the heavens were of old, and the earth standing out of The water and in the water; whereby the world that then was, being overflowed with water, **PERISHED**."

It seem as though the Apostle Peter was referring here not to the Flood, but to the Primeval Earth, which was made "**formless and void**" by a "**Baptism of Water**" that completely submerged it and destroyed all animal life.

Now as the **Framework** of the "Primeval Earth" was not destroyed by its "**Watery Bath**," so the Framework of the "Present Earth" is not to be destroyed by its "**Baptism of Fire**."

This is confirmed by the Apostle's use of the Greek word "Cosmos," which means the "Land surface," the inhabitableness of the earth and not the earth as a planet. It is the exterior surface of the earth then that is to "**Melt With Fervent Heat**" and the "**Works therein Burnt Up**." The intense heat will cause the gases in the atmosphere to explode, which the Apostle describes as the "heavens (the atmosphere) passing away with a **great noise**." The result will be the destruction of all animal and vegetable life, and the alteration of the earth's surface.

The Greek word "**Parerchomai**," which means "**pass away**," doe not mean "**termination of existence**" but means tp pass from "**one condition of existence to another**." The Apostle Paul in his letter to Titus (Titus 3: 5), speaking of the "Regeneration" of men, uses the same word that Jesus used when, in Matt. 19: 28, He promised His disciples that in the "Regeneration," that is in the "**New Earth**," they should sit on "**Twelve Thornes**" judging the "**Twelve Tribes**" of Israel. The word "**Restitution**" in Act 3: 21, means the "**Dissolving**" of which Peter speaks in (II pet. 3: 11), is the same word Jesus used when He said of the colt---"**Loose** him and let him go." The teaching of the scriptures is that "Creation" is at present in a "**state of Captivity**," waiting to be **Loosed from the Bondage** that sin has caused. (Rom. 8: 19-23). It is clear that this earth as a planet is not to be annihilated, but that it is to be Cleansed and Purified by Fire and made fit for the home of those peoples and nations that are to occupy it after its renovation.

This earth that has been consecrated by the presence of the Son of God, where the costliest sacrifice that the universe could furnish was offered up on Calvary to redeem races, for which God has a great future; is too sacred a place to ever be blotted out or cease to exist, for it is the most cherished celestial sphere in the mind of God of all His great creation.

With the "renovation of the Earth by Fire," Time does not end and Eternity begin, for we read in the New Testament of a "**Perfect Kingdom**" that Christ shall surrender to the Father, so that God may be "**All in All**." (I Cor. 15 : 24-28), (Phil. 2: 9-11).

This describes a Kingdom in which all things Celestial, Terrestrial and Infernal are to be subject to the **SON OF MAN**.

Now this "**Perfect Kingdom**" cannot be the "Millennial Kingdom," for that ends in Apostasy and Rebellion; It must therefore mean another Kingdom on the other Side of the "Millennial Kingdom," and as we have seen, there is to be no other Kingdom between the "Millennial Kingdom" and the "Renovation of the Earth by Fire," therefore it must mean a Kingdom that is to follow the "Renovation of the Earth by Fire," and that Kingdom is the Kingdom of the "**New Heaven and the New Earth**," which is called the "**Perfect Kingdom**."

If, as some hold, the "Seventh Day" of the "Creative Week" corresponds to the Millennium, then we have a prophecy of the Dispensation that follows the "Renovation of the Earth" in the "**Morrow After the Sabbath**." (Lev. 23: 36).

The Seventh day of Genesis had to do with the "Old Creation," Which was not finished at that time, for the

Scripture says that the evening and the morning was the first day; and each day afterwards, God added to the creation as He saw fit. but the "**Eighth Day**" has to do with the "**New Creation**," which is perfect, for it was on the "**Eighth Day**," or the "First Day of the week," that our Lord arose from the dead, and 50 days later, on the "**Eighth Day**," that the Holy Spirit was given at Pentecost. Therefore, the "Eighth Day," cannot point to the Millennium, for that is represented by the "Seventh Day," neither can it point to Eternity, for a day is a **Period of Time**, while Eternity is **Timeless**. The "Eighth Day" must then point to a "period of time" between the "Renovation of the Earth" and Eternity, or what we call the "**Perfect Age**." It is also called a dispensation in Eph. 1: 10--- "**The Dispensation of the Fulness of Times**." That is, a "**Full-Time Dispensation**." The intimation is, that all the previous Dispensations were not "Full-Time" Dispensations, that God had to cut them short on account of Sin.

And as the duration of God's Covenant with Israel was extended in Deu. 7: 9 to a "Thousand Generations" or 33,000 years, we have an intimation that the "Dispensation of the Fulness of Times" will last for at least that length of time.

There will be no Sin: All the powers of evil will have been expelled from the earth and imprisoned in the "**Lake of Fire**" forever.

The atmosphere of the New Earth will afford no lurking place for disease germs, for there shall be no more sickness or death, and health will be preserved by the use of the leaves of the "Tree of Life." The heavens shall not robe themselves in angry tempests and somber blackness, nor flash with the thunderbolts of divine wrath, nor cast plagues of hail on the earth, nor cause devouring floods of water or destructive wind storms. It may be that in that day "a Mist shall go up from the earth and water the whole face of the ground" as in Eden, for we read that there shall be ---"**No More Sea**," not that there shall not be large bodies of water, for the river that flows through the street of the New City must have an outlet, but that there shall be no great oceans.

The earth shall also put on its Edenic beauty and glory. There shall no longer be thrones and thistles, no parasites or destructive insects, and labor shall be a delight. No serpents shall hiss among its flowers, nor savage beasts lie in ambush to destroy and devour. Its sod shall not be heaped over newly made graves, nor its soil moistened with tears of sorrow and shame, or saturated with human blood in fratricidal strife. The meek shall inherit the earth, and from north to south, and from east to west, it shall blossom like the rose and be clothed with the verdure of Paradise Restored.

3. THE NEW CITY. (REV. 21: 9—23)

The Angel said to John---"Come hither, I will shew thee the **Bride** the **LAMB'S WIFE**." Some claim that because the word "WIFE" is used here, that Israel instead of the Church, is to be the Bride of Christ. But we must not forget that this offer to show John the Bride, was made after the Wedding of Christ to the Church, and at this time she was no longer the Bride but had become the WIFE of Christ, and should be spoken of as such. But instead of John being shown a Woman, he was shown a CITY, the Holy Jerusalem, and as what makes up a City is not its buildings and parks and business, but its inhabitants, it is clear that the Bride and the City are identical. In other words, the New Jerusalem is the home and residence of the Bride, Remember, Christ married the Church, therefore the Church is the Bride, Jerusalem is the residence of the Bride and is the same as the Bride. From this we see that there is not only to be a **New Heaven** and a **New Earth**, there is also to be a **New City**. This City is the place in John 14: 2—4 where Jesus said He was going back to Heaven to prepare for His Bride the Church.

The description of it is surpassingly grand. It is of Celestial origin. It is not Heaven itself, for it comes down "out of Heaven." No mortal hands are employed in its construction.

It will take up its abode on the New Earth, and this is why this present Earth will have to be renovated by fire, and why there shall be "no more sea," for the New City is 12,000 furlongs, or 1500 square miles, and would reach from Maine to Florida, and from the Atlantic Seaboard 600 miles to the west of the Mississippi River. In other words it would occupy more than one-half of the United States.

The implication is that the length and breadth and the height of it are equal. This is its probable form, for a wall 1500 miles high, and a wall that high would hide the pyramidal part of the City from view. The 144 cubits refered to in Rev. 21: 17 must be referring to the "height" of the wall. For in this wall are 12 gates, 3 on each side, each gate of one Pearl, and these gates are never closed.

The wall itself is of Jasper, and the foundations are garnished with all manner of precious stones. The foundations contain the names of the Twelve Apostles of the Lamb, and over the gates are the names of the Twelve Tribes of Israel.

What a magnificent spectacle such a city must present from a distance with its pyramidal top surmounted by the light of the "**Glory of God**."(Rev. 21: 23, 25). This refers to the City only, and not to the outlying parts of the New Earth, for there will be day and night wherever the light of the City does not reach.

The Pyramidal part of the City will be in the centre of the City, and will not occupy over ½ of the surface area, leaving the remainder to be divided up into boulevards and broad avenues, with numerous parks and residential sections. The City itself is believed to be of **Pure Gold, Like Unto Clear Glass**. (Rev. 21: 18).

Since this refers to the houses and homes of the inhabitants, then the redeemed are to live in palaces of **Transparent Gold**, and the streets are to be of the same material. (Rev. 21: 18, 21).

4. THE NEW NATIONS (REV. 21: 24-27).

This last verse does not imply that there will be sin on the New Earth to endanger the City, but to show that the City will never be contaminated by evil of any kind.

Outside the walls of this beautiful City, spread over the surface of the "New Earth," nations shall dwell, whose Kings shall bring their glory and honor into it, but nothing that will defile or work abomination shall ever enter in through those "Gates of Pearl," for there will be no sin on the New Earth. (Rev. 21: 24—27).

Who Are to be the Happy Inhabitants of This New Earth?

Where did the people who inhabited the earth **after the Flood** come from?

They were the lineal descendants of Noah, how did they escape the flood? They were saved in Noah's Ark which **God Provided.** (Gen. 6: 13—16). Shall not God then during the "Renovation of the Earth by Fire," in some manner, not at this time known; take off righteous representatives of the Millennial nations that He purposes to save, and when the earth is again fit to be the abode of men, place them back on the New Earth, that they may increase and multiply and replenish it, as Adam in Gen. 1: 27, 28, and Noah in Gen. 9: 1, were told to multiply and replenish that present earth.

It is clear from the Scriptures that God does not purpose to create a new race for the New Eart. His promise as to Israel is that the descendants of Abraham shall inherit this earth for a "thousand generations," or 33,000 years; now this is not possible unless they are transplanted into the New Earth. And this is just what God has **Promised**. (Isa. 66: 22).

It seems that from the presence of the Tree of Life in the Garden of Eden, that God intended the human race to populate the Earth, and when it became too thickly populated, to use the surplus population to colonize other spheres. Our "Solar System" is only in its infancy. The Earth is the only one of its planets that as yet is habitable. Where are the inhabitants for the other planets to come from? Do you Thank that the planets of our Solar System, and the planets of other solar systems, of which the stars are the suns, were made simply to adorn the heavens for our little earth. God does not plan things on a Small Scale, and it magnifies His power and wisdom to believe that He created man in His own likeness, a created being higher than the angels, and gifted with the power of Procreation, that He might by means of him populate the Universe. Do you thank that God gave His Son to die on Calvary just to redeem a **few millions** of the human race? God could have blotted them out, as He probably did the Preadamite race, and created a new race, and Satan would have laughed because he had for the second time blocked God's plan for the peopling of this earth.

No, God will not permit Satan to block His plan for peopling this earth with a **Sinless Human Race.** The death of Christ was not merely to redeem a few millions of the human race, but to redeem the **Earth**, and the **Race Itself** from the curse of sin, and the dominion of Satan. The Apostle James tells us in James 1: 18, that we are only the "**First Fruits**" of His "**Creatures**." What then must the **HARVEST BE**?

The Universe is young yet. We are still in the beginning of things, for Isa. 9: 7 says "Of the increase of His government and peace THERE SHALL BE NO END."

When this Earth shall have gone through its "Baptism of Fire," and shall be again fit for the occupancy of man, the representatives of the "Saved Nations" (Rev. 21: 24) will be men and women in whom no taint of sin will remain, and who cannot therefore impart it to their offspring, who will be like the offspring of Adam and Eve would have been if they had not sinned. This magnifies the whole scheme of redemption, and justifies God in the creation of the human race; though God needs no justification.

5. THE NEW RIVER. (REV. 22: 1).

The water of earthly rivers are not crystal clear. Many of them are muddy and contaminated with sewerage. This wonderful river is called the River of the "Water of Life," because of its "life giving" properties. Earthly streams have their source in some mountain spring, but the "River of Life" has its source in the Throne of God. (Rev. 22: 1).

Somewhere on that "Pyramidal Mountain" in the centre of the City, probably on its summit, will rest "**The Thone of God**," from under the seat of which shall flow down in cascades, from terrace to terrace, the crystal stream that shall feed that wonderful "River of Life."

6. THE NEW TREE OF LIFE. (REV 22: 2).

The streets are to be lined with trees, as are also the banks of a wonderful river. These trees are not mere shade trees, but beautiful **Fruit Trees**, called the "**TREE OF LIFE**," that bear **Twelve Kinds of Fruit**, a different kind each month. The fruit of these trees is for overcomers Only.

"To him that **overcometh** will give to eat of the 'Tree of Life' which is in the midst of the Paradise of God." (Rev. 2: 7).

The leaves of the trees are for the **Healing of the Nations that shall** occupy the **New Earth**. Not that there will be any sickness, but to preserve them in health, as Adam would have been preserved in health if he had eaten of the Tree of Life in the Garden of Eden. (Gen. 3: 22-24).

7. THE NEW THRONE (REV. 22: 3-5).

Whoever heard of an earthly city without some place of worship, be it heathen or Christian, but the wonderful thing about the New Jerusalem is, that it has no Temple. Why need a Temple when the object of worship is present, for "The Lord God Almighty and the Lamb Are the Temple of it." In fact the whole City itself will be a Temple. (Rev. 21: 3, 4). This means that Heaven shall have come down to Earth, and that this earth will become the **RESIDENCE OF GOD**.

THE GREAT ABDICATION

The "**Millennial Age**" and the "**Perfect Age**," between which the Earth is Renovated by Fire, make up the "**Age of Ages**," which period is called the **KINGDOM OF THE SON OF MAN**.

At the close of the "Age of Ages" when Christ "shall have put down all rule and all authority and power, for He must reign till He hath put all enemies under his feet," then Christ as the Son of Man, shall surrender the Kingdom to God, that God may be **ALL IN ALL**. (I Cor. 15: 24—28). This is known as **The Great Adbication**.

There have been many abdications of thrones in the world's history, but none like this. Christ will abdicate because He has **Finished the work that was Given Him to Do as the Son of Man**. He will not surrender His Human Nature, but His title "**Son of Man**" will merge back into that of "**Son of God**" so that the Divine Godhead shall thereafter act in its Unity, and God shall be "**ALL IN ALL**."

THE AGES OF THE AGES

As the "Creative Ages" were the "Alpha" Ages, these will be the "Omega" Ages. With the surrender of the "Perfect Kingdom" to the Father, what we speak of as "Time" ceases, and the "Eternal Ages," called the "Ages of the Ages begin. They correspond to what the Apostle Paul in his letter to the Ephesians calls the "Ages to Come." (Eph. 2: 7). And John in the Book of Revelation says that the "Devil" and the "Beast" and the "False Prophet" shall be tormented day and night **forever and ever**, or for the "**Aions**" of the "**Aions**," the "**Ages of the Ages**," (Rev. 20: 10), and that the "Servants of God" shall reign for the same period. (Rev. 22: 5).

What those "Ages of Ages" shall reveal of the Plan and Purpose of God we do not know, but if we are His children, we shall live to know, and possibly take part in their development. What we do know is that we are but in the beginning of things, and as concerning the "Ages," Eternity is still young.

THE EPILOGUE OR FINAL TESTIMONY AND WARNINGS (REV. 22: 6—21).

"And he said unto me. These sayings are faithful and true; and the Lord God of the Holy Prophets sent His Angel to shew unto His Servants the Things which must shortly be done. Behold, I come quickly: blessed is he that Keepeth the sayings of the prophecy of this BOOK. (Rev. 22: 6).

It is important that the readers of "**THIS BOOK**" continue reading Rev. 22: 7-21; to retain the complete understanding of the **PROPHECY OF THE BOOK OF REVELATION: For the time truly is at hand**.

END

OTHER BOOKS BY DR. WILLIAM N. GLOVER S.T.D. THE AUTHOR OF THIS BOOK.

These Books can be purchased by calling English Book Store; 251-478-8535.

SIGNS WONDERS AND MIRACLES

This book shows that Signs, Wonders and Miracles are taking place all of the time.

Just look around, visualize, and observe, God is at work!

FROM ETERNITY TO ETERNITY

The Seven Dispensations of The Bible (Recognized By Most Bible Scholars) are used as a tool to a Clearer Understanding of the entire Bible.

THE THINGS WHICH SHALL
BE AFTER THOSE THINGS

We have now come to the last division of the book. The three Divisions of the book do not overlap nor are they concurrent. The words "after those things" refer to the things that shall immediately follow the completion of the "Church Age," as prefigured in the messages to the Seven Churches. The Church disappears from view with the close of the third chapter of Revelation and is not heard of again until the nineteenth chapter, where her marriage to the Lamb is announced. (Rev. 19: 7-9.)

1. THE HEAVENLY DOOR. (Rev. 4: 1.)

   The scene now changes from earth (Isle of Patmos) to Heaven. John tells us that **after this**, after his vision of Christ in the midst of the "Seven Candlesticks," and his foreview of the history of the Christian Church, which carried him down to the end of the Church Age, he looked and behold a "Door Was Opened in Heaven, and the same voice that spoke to him from the midst of the "seven Golden Candlesticks," which was the voice of Christ (Rev. 1 :10-13), said with the clearness and sweetness of a trumpet--- "**COME UP HITHER AND I WILL SHOW THEE THINGS WHICH MUST BE HEREAFTER.**" And John adds "**IMMEDIATELY I WAS IN THE SPIRIT:** and, behold, a Throne was set in Heaven, and **ONE** sat on the Throne."

2. **. The Things Which "Shall Be after those things."** The "**Things**" which shall come to pass **after** the "Church Period ends. The book of Revelation then divides into **SEVEN SEVENS.**

I.   THE SEVEN CHURCHES. Re 22.
II.   THE SEVEN SEALS. Rev. 6: 1-8 ;
III. THE SEVEN TRUMPETS. Rev. 8: 7-11; 19.
IV. THE SEVEN PERSONAGES. Rev. 12: 1-13 ; 18.
V.   THE SEVEN VIALS Rev. 15: 1- 16 ;21
VI. THE SEVEN DOOMS Rev. 17: 1-20 : 15
VII. THE SEVEN NEW THINGS. Rev. 21: 1-5

GO BACK THIS IS THE END.............................